LOCKED IN

My Imprisoned Years in a Destructive Cult

John Huddle

Survivor Publishing, LLC

Marion, North Carolina

Scripture quotations identified with NIV are from THE HOLY BIBLE, NEW INTERNATIONAL VERSION®, NIV® Copyright © 1973, 1978, 1984, 2011 by Biblica, Inc.® Used by permission. All rights reserved worldwide.

Scripture quotations identified with AMP are from the Amplified® Bible, Copyright © 1954, 1958, 1962, 1964, 1965, 1987 by The Lockman Foundation Used by permission." (www.Lockman.org)

Survivor Publishing, LLC
PO Box 84
Marion, NC 28752
www.survivorpublishing.com

Publisher's Note: This is a true story. Nevertheless, except for the names of prominent Word of Faith Fellowship members, those deceased, and immediate family, all names have been changed to preserve the anonymity of those involved. Names changed for privacy reasons noted with (*). Conversations were composed from memory and presented to reflect the speaker's intentions with the greatest possible accuracy.

Book Layout © 2014 BookDesignTemplates.com

Locked in-John Huddle. -- 1st ed.
ISBN 978-0-9962816-0-7

This book is dedicated to my children, Sarah and Michael. My hopes for you include a life of peace, love, freedom and fulfillment.
I love you, Dad.

CONTENTS

Foreword

How does an idealistic young man with a loving marriage and a sense of spiritual purpose, derived from his Christian faith, become involved in a cult? John was unaware that his local church was affiliated with a church run by an abusive pastor. What he did know was that his local pastor was impressed with this pastor, Jane Whaley, and John was encouraged to move inside Jane's church.

This is an account of how a trusting and innocent person can be vulnerable to the deceptiveness and exploitation of a pastor, whose Christian church had all the elements of a cult. Many cults are deceptive and appear as legitimate organizations at the outset. Members are taken on a step-by-step journey that exposes them to increased manipulation and control over time. If John knew in advance the extent of all that would be required of him, he most likely would have been reluctant to join. Whaley's unique doctrine demanded that members totally conform to her messages from God; and these messages encompassed every aspect of her followers' lives, including family, career, and financial matters, in addition to spiritual concerns.

As with other high demand groups, Jane Whaley had a special vehicle to hook all of her followers into submitting to her ideology. Her hook was loud prayer, which had elements of both positive and negative reinforcement. Loud prayer, an overwhelming experience, used to cast away the ever-present Devil, was utilized to bring Deliverance to straying members. To cope with the bombardment of loud prayer, John retreated and he would lose track of time and disconnect from his feelings, thoughts, and those around him. The deafening sounds and words seemed to take on a life of their own. Whaley reinterpreted the dissociation that loud prayer fostered as a spiritual experience revealing the power of God to cast out the Devil. Another mechanism that kept members on the right path was the desire to avoid the painful onslaught of loud prayer, a vehicle that members were supposed to embrace as "enjoyable."

Other cults use different dissociative processes, such as chanting, meditation, or lecturing. Cult groups employ this bombardment of the senses, plus some degree of isolation from the outside world and restriction of communication within the group, to increase the impact of the cult leader's message. If successful, these techniques move members into a state of intense anxiety and confusion in which they are induced to abandon previous coping mechanisms. Therefore, they inevitably enter into a dissociative state, which is reinterpreted as being some form of a higher power. This belief promotes the members' veneration of the leader and acceptance of the ideas presented. In addition to deception and positive and negative reinforcement, cults also employ group pressure, intimidation, and environmental manipulation. All of this coalesces to develop a new "pseudo-identity" that is formed above the recruit's original personality (West and Martin, 1996, pp. 268-288).

Initially, when filled with doubt, John would remind himself that to have doubts was sinful and, instead, to focus on all he was gaining by his membership. This was how he convinced himself to incorporate his leader's message. Lalich refers to this experience as "bounded choice," two complex processes that occur simultaneously in such situations: conversion and commitment. Lalich states, "There is fusion between the ideal of personal freedom (as promised in the stated goal of the group or its ideology) and the demand for self-renunciation (as prescribed by the rules and norm " (2004, pp. 14-15). In other words, the cult leader demands proof of loyalty to his beliefs; and the cult member believes that, by renouncing his previously held views (which now become devalued), he is attaining the path to purity.

What allowed John to leave? Despite all of this manipulation, after many years, John became increasingly troubled. He saw how Whaley's life contrasted with her followers. In one example of the leader's secrecy, Whaley hid church finances. In one example of hypocrisy, she lived in luxury while she told her followers that to be more spiritual they should not covet worldly pleasures. Instead, they typically shared homes, tithed, and were pressured to spend numerous hours volunteering for the church. Most of all, John began to feel that he was straying away from all that he loved about his Christian faith. Nevertheless, the impetus to leave came when John took the courageous step of refusing to return to an ill suited church run job. It appeared that his better-suited employment, outside of church control, had enabled him to tap into his own desires as separate from God's (Jane's) and rebel against the leadership.

John had a heartbreaking decision to make. Although John felt it was intolerable to remain, the decision to leave was frightening and painful: Members were told that if they leave God's (Jane's) path, they would go to Hell. If John left the church, he would have to leave without his beloved family. Cults destroy the family by interfering with intimacy between family members. Whaley had convinced his family that John was leaving God and his family must shun him in order to get him right with God (Jane).

Outside the cult, John provides support to other former members. He has bravely written his insightful memoir to warn others. Now he lives with the hope that someday those in the group, especially family, would read this book and leave. John Huddle displays warmth, kindness, and humor in his poignant account of the process of enmeshment and extrication from a cult.

Lorna Goldberg, L.C.S.W., Psy.A.
Past President, International Cultic Studies Association
Dean, Institute for Psychoanalytic Studies

Lalich, Janja. (2004). Bounded choice. Berkeley, CA: University of California Press.
Lifton, R. (1961). Thought reform and the psychology of totalism. New York,NY:The Norton Library.

West, L. J. & Martin, P. (1998). Pseudo-identity and the treatment of personality change in victims of captivity and cults. In S.J. Lynn and J. Rhue (Eds.). Dissociation New York, NY: Guilford Press.

Acknowledgements

I want to express my deep appreciation for all of the countless people who have been a part of my story. There is no way to thank each one by name for their contribution of encouragement or instruction or support. If I name some of them, it may put them in a precarious position. The idea for writing this book was born out of the persistent promptings of my mom, Darlene Eichler. She started encouraging me in October of 2008. This is when I began writing my memories of the years in Word of Faith Fellowship. My purpose was to gain clarity and to process the raw emotions of those events. She could see further into the value of my memories and began encouraging me to write a book. I began writing my blog in January 2010 and until February 2014 did not seriously consider the idea of a book. Readers of my blog, friends and other family members also encouraged me through the years. All of them played part in my decision to move forward with this project.

Thanks to my editor, Barbara Evers. She gave me valuable instruction for improvement in my manuscript before I asked her to apply her editing skills. Thanks to my cover designer Marion Johnson. Her creativity and advice made a huge difference. Thank you to all who promised to read this book during the many months it required to finalize this edition.

Winds of Destruction

Severe weather experts reported during the first six months of 2008, *"Tornadoes caused 111 deaths through the end of May, the second highest death toll for any year in the Doppler radar era..."* [1] Though I lived through those months unaware of the death and destruction caused by this severe weather pattern, the winds of destruction blowing in my life during the spring were an ironic reflection of the course of nature's wrath.

April 9, 2008 was a Wednesday.

When running late for a service at Word of Faith Fellowship (WOFF), eating is not a priority. Just get in and take your seat, stay awake, appear interested, take hold and know you are being watched. The end of this evening service brought another meeting for me.

A voice from the podium said, "John Huddle, meet in Ray's office."

My thoughts raced. What had I done? Immediately, I reviewed the last few hours: where, who, what, when, why? Though these meetings were not unusual, after the internal checklist, no alarms went off in my thinking. Many a night was spent in Ray's office after a church service planning, reviewing and managing the next crisis for my employer, Two Mile Properties.

The first awareness of a strange breeze blowing occurred when I saw my wife standing outside the office door in the fellowship hall. She was as nervous as a bridled filly waiting to jump and run. Her nervousness should have sounded a loud alarm, but I missed it.

I asked, "Why are you here? Where are the children?"

"The children are taken hold of," she answered avoiding my gaze at every point.

Martha's name had not been called. Wading through the hallway hustle and bustle, that narrow artery teaming with children and adults moving along their chosen path, my thoughts caught a glimpse of the hidden truth--she knew the purpose of the meeting. Her expression portrayed angst and yet, I was unsure.

"Will you be in this meeting?"

Her nod sent uneasiness into the pit of my stomach.

Not a business meeting. Sirens wailed. Thoughts bombarded my mind, waves of fear washed over me leaving their residue. Why did the owners call my wife into this meeting?

Even then, it was hard to accept one of the "living mantras" of WOFF: Each part of your life is subject to "the will of God." In order to know and live in "the will of God," every part of your life is inter-connected and subject to the ever-changing, more intrusive and far-reaching control dynamics of WOFF as administered by the leader— Jane Whaley. She heard God for everyone—reaching into every part of your life. "Sin in your life" kept you from knowing God's will.

The next few hours changed my life in ways only known by Providence.

Time seemed suspended while I stood outside the office door. As a leader in the church, Ray had an office that served many purposes. Soon, he approached in his slow and deliberate fashion. He sported a look which was meant to put me at ease. I recognized his gentle nature when he brought truth to someone. We exchanged greetings as he unlocked the door and motioned for us to come inside. I took a seat in a small corner at the front of the desk. My wife stood at my left side as he made motions for more folks to crowd into the room. Josh F. took the seat behind the desk. As an attorney and owner of Two Mile, his words carried weight. During the short awkward exchanges of those filing in, it quickly became evident that everyone else had been briefed about the proceedings.

Those in attendance included former pastors of the Greenville church, Gerald Southerland, and his wife, Linda. He had a tall frame, and his head was capped with perfect hair. His low key demeanor made him easy prey for Jane's grip. Linda prospered in this matriarchal subculture by using obedience pushed by an underlying destructive self-loathing. My wife and I first came in contact with WOFF through their Greenville church in 1992.

Andy K., my immediate supervisor at Two Mile entered the room looking assured of his purpose. Andy, an intelligent and deliberate fellow, never ignoring the levels of authority inside WOFF, however at times, he showed flashes of self desire betraying his shiny coat

About 9:30PM, Ray led off with a why we are all here statement "Josh brought some things to my attention that pertain to you."

Josh took the lead in a much stronger fashion. "If I had known what was going on earlier, I would have addressed this sooner. Andy tells me that you have been spending too many hours on your part-time Credit Union work; your focus has been more on that than with Two Mile."

This statement made me think this was an extension of an impromptu meeting back in March when Andy confronted me about my trust and loyalty. Wrongly, I assumed the fallout from that meeting had been averted.

All in attendance remained solemn waiting for Josh to finish and for me to react to his assessment. His ending ultimatum included, "…tonight, you will quit your part-time job or you will be fired from Two Mile Properties."

Life inside WOFF required synergy. My part-time Credit Union work remained a sticking point for years in the group's quest to own me. This position left me "out from under authority."

My response to Josh included an awkward silence as I considered an acceptable and accurate reply. "I have a real problem with that."

This initial refusal to accept Josh's assessment as the will of God brought the next level of reviews of my worth as a person. Andy spoke up next pointing out a time when I left the job to pay a bill. Yes, I did, but with all the hours I put in, I felt justified to take some time for personal business. That answer did not stop their fury; it sent the personal rebukes to a new level.

About this time, Brooke C. arrived. She blew into the room; her position of leadership included a level of authority surpassing all others in the room. The length of this meeting instantly extended to indefinite. Brooke announced, "There must be the unclean in your life since you could not immediately accept and embrace 'the will of God' for the job change."

The scope and pace of the accusations increased at this point. Moving from job related infractions to my intimate relationship and private time with my wife. We were registering at least an EF-3 on the tornado scale. Their demands increased in an attempt to elicit a confession of whatever sin obviously resided in my heart.

"What is it, John? What is the sin so deep which you have hidden for years that is taking you over?

"That sin is blinding you to God's will, right now! Tell us, let us blast it and get you help…"

"Whatever it is, it is holding you back from taking your place …."

"We love you, you know that. We want to help you…"

Brooke summed up the barrage, "If you were right with God, you would be able to accept the will of God, immediately, no matter what."

The session continued. Brooke and the others took turns berating and pounding me in an effort to open my heart and make me confess my sin. Once a new accusation was pronounced, everyone stared and waited for me to confess to something.

During these silent stare sessions, I drifted into a dream-like state. The people chattered around me, but my understanding slowed. Any response I did give had to be forced from my mouth. I knew the wrongness surrounding this whole scene, yet I felt powerless to change or stop it. With all that was in me I wanted to forget this night all together and get up and run.

During this dream-like state, I realized each person in the room believed the way I was treated was normal and acceptable. Later, that realization became the seed of strength which grew and caused me to leave WOFF.

After about ninety minutes, I did what I later learned other survivors did under the same circumstances. I agreed and confessed something in hopes to end the onslaught. In hindsight, I know the subject of my confession didn't matter. Obtaining a confession cemented me deeper under their control.

After this useless admission, Jane Whaley stormed in the room, poked her finger in my obviously confused face and screamed, "You are full of the unclean!"

At that point, in unison, those around me blurted out, "You cut your eyes at her! That was a devil!"

Suddenly, memories of other members telling about their moments like this flooded my mind. They talked of meeting the "authority of God." Up until then, I had no idea what they were saying. Never had my inner personal space been invaded as much as in this meeting. The sea of activity spun out of control as I clung to my racing thoughts seeking shelter and finding none.

Next, Jane turned on my crying wife, "And you let him be this way!"

Jane left the gathering muttering she had other meetings.

My wife, catching the spirit of the EF-5 blowing through the room began screaming at me, "Repent and start crying out to God!"

At that exhortation, my hopes to end this trauma session rested on leaning over and doing my best to at least feign some behaviors accepted by WOFF as repentance. I knew it to be shallow at best, since the dream-like session left me past feeling, as if under a dose of anesthesia. I retreated into the inner part of my being while watching this horror movie unfold around me. Even my hearing lessened and some rebukes had to be repeated.

After two and a half hours, I still refused to give in to the screaming, rebukes and WOFF reasoning. Brooke reached for the phone calling for Jane's direction, "Jane, we are not getting anywhere here, I think we need to quit."

Once she uttered, "Okay," and hung-up, the meeting broke up. So odd; no one else seemed affected in the least by the winds of destruction that had blown me over.

My wife asked Josh, "Does he go to work on Thursday?"

By this time, Josh was in the hallway. "I don't need anyone like that working for me."

And with that answer, I was fired. I surrendered the company car and the laptop.

The rolling drama did not end when I left the church grounds. After a solemn ride home with my wife, the children already in bed, my wife exclaimed, "You don't sleep in this bed."

Shell shocked, I slept in the recliner. Honestly, who wanted to be next to her at that time?

I remember waking up the next morning to an empty feeling. Was it all a dream? Would things go back to normal and mend themselves? No. The destruction set on course by the tornado force winds that blew into my life was real. The damage was only beginning to be felt.

I lived through Hurricane Hugo in 1989 and had experienced the aftermath. Thursday was the morning after the storm. The damage assessment began. I spent the day wandering, wondering and thinking, *What if things were different? Can we fix this? What do I do from here?* Though I could not see into the future, my world had forever changed.

By the next night, I gathered my courage telling my wife "I am sleeping in my bed. If you don't like it, you can sleep in the recliner." We slept in the bed on our separate edges, not touching. No doubt, after that evening, our relationship was on a downhill slide.

April 9th marked our twentieth wedding anniversary.

PART ONE

FROM THE BEGINNING

CHAPTER ONE

SMALL TOWN TRADTIONS

Memories of my youth include many happy and joyous times. Life in the small town of Dublin, Virginia was simple and in many ways typically southern. Our family of six lived on Maple Street with my Dad working for a division of the Federal Government and my Mom spending time in the local school system as a teacher and librarian. I enjoyed life with my parents, two sisters and brother in Dublin. My years there included running a paper route, and participating in Boy Scouts, the church youth group and sports activities after school. During my high school years, I experienced the typical joys and dramas of teenage life. My life reflected pure Americana.

My parents' grew up in a nearby community, and many of my extended family still lived there during my youth. We attended several family events and experienced a warm history of holiday celebrations and special family gatherings. I visited often with my grandparents, uncles, aunts and cousins. While spending the weekends with my grandparents, I attended church with them. In the summers, we attended Vacation Bible School and other special meetings in that community.

As many young folks do, I wandered away from my family heritage during my college years. In 1984, I started asking questions and expressed an interest in Christianity. I attended a small church in

Summerville, SC. After a few months, I transitioned to a non-denominational church about an hour away in the Beaufort area. The people were warm and seemed to take their faith seriously. I continued attending there and spent many Sundays driving back and forth. Eventually, I started teaching a Bible study during the week for those who lived a distance from the church.

By 1985, my search for work took me to Lexington, SC. Regardless of the distance; on most Sundays, I made the trip to Beaufort.

Soon, I was hired as an outside representative with a large automobile finance company. This position required that I travel out of town several nights a week. I spent many hours on the road. Sundays were no different. When I first arrived in Lexington, I lived in a small house in the middle of town. After a few months, I took in a roommate named Steve*. Steve attended a local church and had developed several friendships.

Somewhere in our conversations over ice cream, he said, "I know this girl you need to meet. Her name is Martha."

"I have no interest in meeting her."

For a time, I wanted to experience being single. Though his persistence did not annoy me, more than once I dodged his prearranged rendezvous. Every time I refused his invitations, he laughed his memorable cackle and smiled. "John, you are something."

By the end of 1986, my decision to move out left Steve in the house and led me to a small two bedroom apartment. Soon after that my brother moved in with me. We used these weeks to catch up on the missed years after I left home to attend college. Our time together included simple walks to the store for a cold drink or an ice cream. December of 1986 holds no special memories. My brother and I lived that month one day a time.

Unbeknownst to me, January 1st of 1987 held the beginning of a whole new direction for my life.

CHAPTER TWO

NEW YEAR POSSIBILITIES

Early on January 1, I called a friend named Tina* who lived on the other side of Lexington. I met her through Steve and wanted her to meet my brother. At the appointed time, I knocked on the door and walked into Tina's apartment with my brother not far behind. There sitting on the couch was a young lady I did not know. She seemed engrossed in something, but turned and looked my way.

Tina opened the conversation, "John, this is Martha. She moved in a few days ago." At last, despite my efforts, I encountered Martha.

The small townhome smelled like orange spice, the scent coming from a mixture simmering on the stove. Tina's spastic dog bounced about the box-filled room.

"Oh, you are Martha."

"Oh, you are John."

We exchanged nervous smiles. She was petite with curly hair and a contagious smile. After the rush of embarrassment and uneasiness wore off, she talked with enthusiasm. We cautiously exchanged bits of information about each other.

"So, Martha, where did you live before here?"

"I shared an apartment in Columbia off Broad River Road."

"Where do you work?"

"I work for an attorney on the West side. Well, I also work for his wife, helping her."

This is going good. She is smiling back. I wonder if that means something. No, I am sure it doesn't.

Martha continued, "I went to Oral Roberts University for a couple of years, but I'm back now, taking a break. John, what do you do?"

"I visited ORU a few years back on family vacation. I work for a large national auto finance company as an outside representative. Translated, I check automobile dealer floor plans and repossess cars."

We laughed at the idea of me having a job repossessing cars.

Wow, that went well. Usually folks cringe or make a snide comment when I tell them about my work.

Tina had Christian music playing on her stereo.

"Do you like this group, John?"

"Yes, I listen to them a lot. Do you?"

"Yes, I saw them in Charlotte. I'm from Rock Hill."

She talked openly of her Christian faith while telling me about a couple she recently met who were missionaries. She promised to introduce me.

Not long after my brother and I arrived, Tina suggested cooking a meal. Amidst the spastic fits from Tina's dog, we prepared dinner while continuing the conversation. We learned that Steve was telling her about me, and all the while he was coaching me about her.

I was not interested in pursuing a relationship. There were too many pitfalls and too much drama in that arena. I truly had no interest. That decision allowed me to enjoy the encounter. We were going to be friends. Besides, I was five whole years older. That felt like a lot.

Exactly how long we stayed, I don't remember. Suffice it to say that by the weekend, Martha rode with my brother and me to church in Beaufort. Two weeks later, she baked me some of her famous chocolate chip cookies and left them at my front door. Within another few weeks, I cleaned her Plymouth Volare® station wagon. Things were moving faster than I planned. She offered to clean my apartment, I let her. My brother was shocked. Later that winter, I showed her how to drive her car in the snow.

A few days after our first meeting, I dropped by Steve's house.

"Steve, guess who I met the other day at Tina's?"

"No, tell me you didn't."

"Yes, I finally met Martha, she's living with Tina."

"John, I told you!"

He let out a belly laugh that shook the walls. He had a grin that did not quit.

In February, despite a snow storm, we drove to her parents in Rock Hill. We enjoyed crock pot spaghetti and great conversation. Her parents were friendly, down home folks, concerned about their daughter and yet polite to me. The need to travel back in bad weather caused us to cut our visit short. As we were leaving, she quipped to her Mom, "Don't worry. He's just a friend."

Her Mom let out a roll of laughter, "Yes, right."

The months that followed were full of courtship around a common interest of Christian faith and church activities. During the summer, we drove back to her parents, and I asked them to go to the park. I planned for them to take a walk with me, without Martha. After some small talk, I got to the point.

"Would you be surprised if I said I wanted to marry your daughter?"

After the laughter subsided, her parents answered, "We are not shocked."

Her father asked us to do three things before we married. First, wait a year. Second, listen to a set of tapes by Dr. Ed Cole on the marriage relationship and lastly, meet with Gerald and Linda Southerland. Her parents trusted the judgment of Gerald and Linda and considered them as their pastors from their years spent in Spartanburg, SC, before they moved to Rock Hill. Her parents contributed to the Southerland's ministry and received cassette tapes of the Sunday sermons.

I agreed and started the countdown.

The months passed quickly. My work took me out of town several nights a week, so we agreed to spend time together on the weekends. Soon the appointed time to meet Gerald and Linda Southerland in Greenville arrived, January 1988. By this meeting, Martha's parents had given in on the requirement to wait a year. The wedding date was set for April 9th.

I remember the day as cold and clear. We met the Southerlands at their church, a traditional church building with stained glass windows and pews. After the introductions and hugs, Martha went in one direction with Linda, and I went with Gerald to another room. Gerald's gift of conversation became evident. He did not know me but made me feel welcome and important in this brief encounter. I can't remember the questions, but I must have passed the test. At the conclusion, Gerald and Linda confirmed, in our presence, that they saw no reason why we should not be married. We floated back to Lexington and continued with our plans.

The wedding was on.

CHAPTER THREE

NEW BEGINNINGS

During the first few months of 1988, I moved to Beaufort and stayed with a kind family in the church. Preparations continued for the big day. Soon, we found a place of our own to live. After a simple wedding with lots of children around and a weeklong honeymoon in Charleston, we settled into the life of newlyweds.

Before the wedding, I secured a job with a consumer finance company in Beaufort. Martha found work at an area car dealership. We lived near the Air Force Base in a small blue doublewide trailer. Humble beginnings, but we were happy. Settling in to a routine involved the normal give and take any couple worked through. We made it through those first few months.

Living this close to the church meant no more long Sunday drives. By the end of the year, we agreed to move to Charleston with a couple from the church as they started a new ministry. We harbored hopes of one day being 'in the ministry' ourselves. Moving and helping our friends establish their ministry may one day lead us in that direction. We finally sold our place and moved into the living room of Sidney and Pat Haynes*. We stayed for a few weeks until I found work at my first Credit Union in North Charleston. The pay was meager, but it allowed us to move into a townhouse in West Ashley. We stayed close to the Haynes and became involved in their church.

We lived in this townhouse when Hurricane Hugo struck Charleston in September of 1989. The week before Hugo arrived is etched in my memory. Between Monday evening and Tuesday morning before the storm, I decided the storm would be too great. We were leaving. We planned to evacuate to Rock Hill and be with Martha's parents.

The Tuesday morning before that fateful day, the employees of the Credit Union were finishing a staff meeting in the lobby of the main branch. I asked the President if there were any special plans for the possibility of Hugo hitting the city. He scoffed and dismissed my questions with a resounding expression of doubt. This rebuff happened a little before 9:00AM. By the next evening, the 6 o'clock news carried a live broadcast of the Emergency Preparedness Director issuing a recommended evacuation notice. The mandatory evacuation would not be issued until 6AM the next morning.

What I heard that evening was *get out of town!* Never before had I faced a crisis of this serious nature. Every decision we made was critical. I asked my neighbor's help in moving the furniture to the second floor of our townhouse. Electricity was in the air!

Wednesday passed as a slow blur full of what ifs. Early Thursday morning, September 21st, my wife and I attended a prayer vigil at Pastor Frank Dane's* church in West Ashley. As soon as the prayer ended, I declared, "Stay of you want, but we are leaving."

The next morning there was several feet of water covering the floor in the building where we prayed. The Pastor needed a boat to get to his church.

For the mandatory evacuation, authorities closed the lanes leading into Charleston on I-26 and directed traffic outbound in all four lanes. Shortly after noon, my wife and I made our way onto the crowded entrance ramp of I-26. She drove our car, while I drove the credit union's van. A trip that normally took three hours lasted five. At times, the traffic was at a complete standstill. I rolled down the window listening to the sounds of radios in other vehicles repeating the evacuation warnings. The pungent exhaust fumes from the massive move of thousands leaving the Charleston area were memorable indeed. The skies were almost clear, just a few high clouds, signaling the dangers to come in the next few hours.

We stopped at the Credit Union branch in Orangeburg to drop off the computer back-up tapes. My wife and I were still in preparation mode for a hurricane when we reached Rock Hill. We rushed to the store to buy duct tape and batteries while others in line purchased ice cream and fresh meats. The folks around us were relaxed, but we felt keyed up by the events playing out in Charleston. We used duct tape on the windows of my wife's parent's home even though there were no warnings issued for that area.

Late that evening, Hugo made a direct hit over downtown Charleston. Residents, who stayed and survived, swore never again, they were not riding out another storm. Early the next morning, Hugo surprised everyone as it headed into the area around Charlotte, NC. Wakened from a shallow sleep, it sounded like a freight train in the front yard. My mother-in-law was up watching the reports on her small battery-powered television. At that moment, we were grateful we taped the windows. Many in the area were without power for two weeks or longer.

Over the weekend following the storm, the efforts to secure the basics such as ice, fresh water and other drinks took most of the daylight hours. The grocery stores were without electricity. Shoppers were escorted, a few at a time, with flashlights and paying with cash was preferred. We stayed in Rock Hill until the following Monday. Nothing could prepare us for the scenes we witnessed in Charleston. Somewhere south of Orangeburg, we began to notice the damage. Groves of pine trees all snapped off at the height of about fifteen feet as if a large chainsaw cut them. I-26 was mostly clear, the damage more noticeable the closer we came to Charleston. As we approached the bridge to cross the Ashley River, to our left was a three story dry dock storage facility in a heap. Boats were laying on top of each other two and three deep. The steel supports of the building's frame bowed over pointing downward. The scenes seemed surreal as if we were visiting a city on another planet. As we drove to our townhouse, we breathed a sigh of relief. Our home only lost a few shingles and had no water damage. We were stunned and grateful. Our neighbors dealt with trees through their roof in their living room or bedroom.

For two weeks, we suffered with no electricity. The water smelled like pine sap because of the downed trees landing in the main water source. There were news reports covering the damages and warnings to stay away from the barrier islands, but we could not watch them on our television. We went to bed early, listening to our small battery-powered AM radio. Radios were important for learning the locations of free supplies such as fresh water, toiletries, canned goods and other staples.

The devastation of the natural world around us was only an indicator of the emotional and internal trauma this disaster created on many in the area. Homes and businesses were lost. Researchers recorded about six hundred small businesses that folded as a result of Hugo.. The lines for water and free supplies were long. In the midst of the recovery, I learned of folks storing up supplies which were not immediately needed and could go to ones in true need. This confused me. Some had the attitude, if it's free, let's go get our share. I saw what folks do under extreme pressures and will never forget those lessons.

With 1989 behind us, we entered a year of changes in our lives, 1990. Our daughter, Sarah Elizabeth was born November 13th. When we came home with our new baby girl, my mother-in-law stayed with us for a few weeks. It took weeks before I realized how much we both benefited from her kindness. The irony of geologists recording an earthquake that day was not lost on us. We learned so much as new parents. Through the changes, our lives were enriched by the needs and joys around our daughter. As the days turned into weeks and months, we grew together as a family.

CHAPTER FOUR

TOO MUCH OF A GOOD THING

Through the end of 1990 and into 1991, we served in a small church in Summerville, SC. The church had many needs, and my wife and I were willing to jump in and help. This eagerness was to our spiritual detriment. By December of 1991, the burden of activity left us searching for understanding and relief from the overload. The people were sweet, the Pastor was grateful to have the help, but we were not mature enough to allow others to step in and share the load. The excitement of service overran the good sense to keep priorities in order. Martha was helping with secretarial duties and I helped with teaching classes, and organizing the youth group. Soon, we were overcommitted and bewildered at the loss of joy and enthusiasm.

We contacted Martha's parents and asked them for some tapes, thinking we needed a fresh perspective. They gave us a series preached by Gerald Southerland, entitled "Dealing with the Issues of the Heart." In a few days, after listening to the tapes, we called to ask them if Gerald and Linda Southerland were willing to talk to us. We needed to find clarity in the joyless spiritual daze. We accepted an invitation to meet with Gerald and Linda to discuss our predicament. Early one Sunday morning in January 1992, we packed our small Honda and headed to Greenville, SC. For the trip, we used directions from Martha's dad since he visited there on business. Leaving before dawn, our plan was to arrive about 9:30AM. We approached the exit off I-85 about 9:20AM.

We turned left off the ramp and started searching; not knowing the exit roads had changed since my father-in-law last made the trip. We were headed in the wrong direction.

Sunday morning was not the best time to ask for directions. Many businesses were closed. After three or four turns and folks returning blank stares to our questions, we were exasperated and about to give up. Somehow, we learned that the exit had changed and managed to find the correct road. Finally, we found the two double wide trailers in the open field which served as the church facilities. We pulled into the parking lot, seeing puffs of steam rolling from under the hood of our car. The car's radiator issues were no surprise. It was a very 'used' car. We left it to cool agreeing to worry about it after the service. We slipped in the second row beside Greg and Suzanna Southerland.

Greg whispered, "We thought you weren't coming."

I replied, "We got lost and the car overheated."

I don't remember what was preached, I don't remember who was in attendance. What I do remember is the super friendly attitude and over joyous welcome. A member of the church fixed our car after the service. Then, Gerald and Linda, along with several of their members, escorted us to a local restaurant. There were cordialities along with some timely questions. One subject intrigued both of us. Gerald and Linda taught a "Word of Life Training Center" Monday through Friday during the morning. There was no set schedule of subjects. Prayer was first, and then they taught "as God leads." We found out later that students took notes which were handed in to Linda for her to grade. It all sounded informal, yet serious. Martha and I had expressed our desire to "be in the ministry" for several years.

After lunch, we piled back into our small car making our way back to Summerville. A moment of silence, filled with expectation, settled over us in the car.

In a moment burned in my memory, we drove toward the intersection for Highway 14. At a strip-shopping center with a Bi-Lo grocery store directly across from us. I paused for an extra few seconds. Martha looked at me waiting for me to speak.

"I think we need to get a paper…we might be moving up here."

Martha nodded her cautious agreement. We pulled into the shopping center to buy the local paper. On the way home, she read the want ads for places to live and a possible job for me. The trip home seemed faster than the morning ride. Our ties to Summerville weakened with the possibility of a new spiritual start with a church that "trains people to be ministers." The idea of pursuing this elusive goal with folks Martha had known for years was inviting and magnetizing at that moment. After all, everyone was so nice, loving and friendly. This had to be the next step, right? God seemed to be leading us. We made this decision before seeing and experiencing the main signature practices of the church in Greenville, and we knew nothing about Word of Faith Fellowship in Spindale, NC.

CHAPTER FIVE

NEW FRIENDS, NEW FRIENDS, NEW PRACTICES

During the next visit to the church, we heard Greg play the drums and saw "blasting prayer." This was not the first time hearing drums in a church service. That part was not unusual. The people standing or walking around doing "blasting prayer" was new.

In years past, I had read of "moves of God" where people stood up or laid down for hours in a trance. I read of meetings where many fell down weeping and crying out for mercy. In meetings led by Charles Finney, an evangelist from many years ago, people cried out loudly for God's mercy. Could this be one of those spiritual happenings like I had read about? Many of the people's face appeared angry and their fingers pointed up to the ceiling as if to aim at something or someone. Yet, as quick as they were angry, they turned and glanced my way and smiled. Many of the words they spoke were not words at all, just long drawn out syllables. It was confusing and loud, but I did not scoff or doubt at this point. If it was real, I wanted to learn. This seemed awkward, but I wanted to know more. After all, these folks were "training to be in the ministry." I needed to know.

In reality, by then, we were committed in our hearts. We had many questions about this new "blasting prayer." A few of the questions: Where is it in the Bible? What does it do for you? How do you do it?

Why do you move your hands like that? The answers were found in the Scriptures we were told. Look here in Isaiah, look here in Psalms and pray about it. "Carry it."

During our initial conversations, we learned that several families in the church lived in shared housing. This practice was "God's way." We traveled to Greenville a few more times staying weekends with a couple in the church, Manley and Lora Bonar*. They lived with three children in shared housing. The Bonars explained the practices of the church. This new mentoring relationship lasted many years.

At the end of March, we planned to move into a small blue house on Highway 101 on the outskirts of Greer. The days leading to the move were filled with excitement and anxious thoughts. *Where would I find work? What if...? What if not...?* It all felt like a dream, yet, at times, it felt so right. We were moving hours away from friends we had known for years, but all the positive thoughts about this move seemed sufficient to override any doubt.

The day arrived. We rented a large yellow truck and packed it full. That morning we ate breakfast with friends who encouraged us to stay. We explained our desires to move and become a part of the church in Greenville. Though I did not admit it, I experienced a tinge of apprehension, leaving the familiar and striking out to the north. We pulled out of the parking lot, pressing on. We drove out of Summerville, the small brown Honda packed to the gills. The excitement was palpable. This move may bring us "into the ministry," our elusive goal. Try as we may, the meaning and method to fulfill it had escaped us. Could this decision lead to the attainment of that goal?

After several hours, we arrived to a welcome committee of several gracious church members at the small blue house. Smiles, hugs and helping hands made the unpacking go smoothly. The church members bought us a stove as a welcome gift. Such a surprise!

After getting the beds set-up and some of the dishes put away, we began life as a part of Grace and Truth Fellowship. All of our boxes did not fit into the little house, so we left them stacked in the yard.

The clean freshly painted house had less space than we realized. In the months to come, we learned we did not need a lot of the "stuff" in those boxes. Much of it tied us to our past and we were moving on, in the call of God. It was all a process. There was so much to learn.

The activities of Grace and Truth Fellowship centered around two double wide trailers on Batesville Road. The first trailer had an open floor plan and served as the sanctuary. The second one divided into an office and classrooms for the school, Grace Christian Academy. At first glance, the surroundings appeared meager: two large, double-wide, manufactured buildings surrounded by a gravel parking lot in the middle of a field. We did not notice. We focused on the warmth of the people and new knowledge yet to be learned.

Martha took a position helping in the school. Our daughter started in the school at eighteen months. She loved it. I attended the Training Center in the mornings and found work at a pizza business working second shift. Later, I also worked on contract for the same Credit Union I had worked for in Charleston. They built a branch in Greenville right beside the pizza place.

Finances were tight, but we were involved in the adventures of a new life in a new group of friends. We sold things using the local paper and put on a yard sale or two. Helpful, kind members anonymously left food for us at our car after the services. At first, accepting these gifts proved difficult. As time passed, we became grateful for them.

A normal week for me included attending the Training Center in the mornings. We began with prayer for an hour or so. Next, Linda or Gerald taught on various subjects, all of which were related to the "move of God" we were in. Subjects included submission to spiritual authority, deliverance, forms of prayer including loud prayer, and warnings about the devil's attacks against us. At times, other students were encouraged to stand up and share their understanding of scriptures. We ended around noon. After lunch, I worked in the afternoon and evenings. Occasionally, I attended the prison ministry at Dutchman Correctional Institution with Gerald and Greg. We attended Tuesday evening prayer service and mid-week services on Thursday evenings. Saturdays included working and chores around the house.

Once a month, in a member's home, the church held a "marriage circle" meeting. Gerald and Linda led these covered dish meetings, helping couples "get ahold of God" in their marriages and their families. At first, I felt uncomfortable in these meetings. Even though we were getting to know the other members, it felt as if we were interrupting a close knit group with many rules about acceptable and unacceptable behaviors.

Looking back that is exactly what was happening. These meetings were used to correct behaviors or institute new understandings of God's ways between husband, wife and the children. You soon learned acceptable dress, manners and speech. I found it best to listen and watch others to learn what was acceptable. To me, these meetings were intense for that reason. This monthly meeting was considered as vital as the Sunday morning worship service. If you missed one, "you missed God's will for your life."

On Sundays, church services filled the time from the morning into early afternoon. There was no Sunday evening service at that time.
The church continued to help us in our financial struggles. Later in that year, I obtained a part-time position with another credit union in Spartanburg.

Many of the church practices, including the blasting prayer, were new to me. At times, the extent of the new customs seemed overwhelming. I had questions. When I asked, they directed me to certain Scriptures and told me to "carry it and pray about it" and God would show me.

As we adjusted to life in this church, questions of doctrine and practice had to be answered. Gerald and Linda taught that Christians could have "devils," therefore, they needed deliverance. This opened the way for all folks, Christian or not, to need deliverance. If you were having troubles, more often than not a devil was after you, in you, around you or upon you. Maybe the folks you were around were carrying those devils and releasing them at you with their thoughts or their actions or their music or their touch or their looks or their words about you or something in their house, or someone in their family or someone in their past...

You get the picture.

Tuesday night meetings were filled with prayer circles, loud, blasting, deliverance prayer, coughing into paper towels and putting the used paper towels in piles in the floor. Later, we put them in the plastic dish pans.

During the prayer, the small building warmed up quickly. Fans were placed in the church, but, the emphasis was not on the physical temperature but on getting your deliverance and helping others do the same. We were all in this thing together.

As weeks passed, we learned the church operated with two internal groups, leadership and non-leadership. Leadership met before services in Gerald's office to "get ahold of the service." Non-leadership arrived and sat in the sanctuary until the meeting in Gerald's office ended. The services started after that meeting. I was not in the leadership meetings and cannot say what happened there. From my observation, the leadership group consisted of young couples who were willing to repeat the doctrine and do "the work of the ministry." That made them leadership.

As I reflect, I know I wanted to be accepted and not thought of as a non-spiritual fool. For reasons, some known and some unknown, I wanted to believe these new practices were right and true. So, I chose to act it until I could believe it. Martha had known Gerald and Linda since her mid-teens. I believed they were not leading us astray. They were further along in the things of God than us. After all, we were only beginning to learn about the ways of God: deliverance, loud prayer, also referred to as blasting, living in households, hearing by the Spirit, living by the Spirit, and all of these folks were deep in it. I wanted to be accepted and I made the answers fit the questions. Can you see the pattern?

This process proved a big mistake in the years to come.

We moved to Greenville at the end of March. April passed quickly, and we began to hear about the May seminar at Word of Faith Fellowship. There was no doubt we would attend. This seminar was a weeklong series, meeting three times a day, where Jane Whaley and her ministry team shared what God was doing. They emphasized teaching the ways of God for everyday life.

As time went on, we learned these new doctrines and practices at Grace and Truth originated with Jane and Sam Whaley. Gerald and Linda had reconnected with Sam and Jane a few years earlier and had gone to Spindale for their "deliverance." This experience changed their outlook on ministry and, as a result, reduced their church from over four hundred members to about one hundred. Many members did not accept many of the new practices imported from Spindale. Gerald explained the ones who had left were ones who wanted to keep their devils, keep their sin, etc. At the time, I could not imagine why anyone wanted to leave this place.

At WOFF, Jane ran the show. She heard God at a level no one else could and according to her, everyone else was full of devils. She preached loud and prayed louder. While in the first few services, it was difficult to accurately know just how far reaching her controls extended. From watching other WOFF members, it appeared everyone else considered Jane's demeanor and role as normal. I had never witnessed a minister with this level of sway and influence. Again, I wanted to be accepted, so I kept many of my opinions to myself, waiting to see how this all worked out. There were more reasonable moments during the services and to those I clung. The meetings at the first seminar were held at 9:00AM, 2:00PM and 5:00PM. Leadership meetings were before the evening meeting. WOFF never printed a bulletin to let anyone know what to expect. Each service occurred as Jane heard God, and we followed.

WOFF included a Bible School at the time. The classes were held in the mornings. Jane and other leadership taught classes using the Amplified Bible as the text. The sessions often included deliverance prayer. There were students attending from many different countries. Students were told to believe God for their financial support. This meant they had to pay their own way, often working jobs in the afternoon and evenings.

In May of 1992, the upper field where the Word of Faith Christian School stands now was a dirt field used for parking. We stayed in a hotel for the first seminar in 1992, and a few times afterwards when attending seminars. It required a lot of planning to keep a small child in a hotel for a week. Most times, we took our small refrigerator. Later, we stayed in member's homes during seminar week. This opened a whole new level of "living with God's people." We saw the good and the areas where members were still learning Gods' ways.

CHAPTER SIX

ANOTHER STEP IN GOD'S WILL, RIGHT?

One day in the small blue house, Martha and I were eating lunch. It was probably pizza; we lived on it during the first few months. Sitting across from each other at a small table, I finished asking her a question and waited for a reply. Martha said nothing, but started swinging her arms and using her hands similar to a church practice known as "blasting."

I blurted, "You may not agree with me, but you did not have to blast me like that!

She laughed, "John, I was swatting the gnats!"

We laughed and continued eating our pizza. In this new world, we were learning to communicate.

Our time in the blue house lasted six months. We were then invited to live with Greg and Suzanna Southerland in their home on Governor's Square in Greer. We considered it for about three minutes, deciding this must be the next step in knowing God's ways. Greg and Suzanna's home included a great room and kitchen in the middle between bedrooms on each end. They lived in the master bedroom with their own bathroom. We lived in the other end with two bedrooms and a separate bathroom. There was a large deck with a fenced-in backyard. The house was a cute and functional home. In this cozy setting, we began our household adventure of living God's way.

In our new household, we split the cost of groceries and utilities, and paid rent. To help with our struggles, as a kindness, Greg and Suzanna helped us financially until we paid what we owed.

Moving into the Southerland household had its advantages and disadvantages. We were by daily association closer to all of the Southerlands, and we saw things that other church members did not. After being there only a few weeks, we were privileged to experience a behind-the-scenes drama. I know now these scenes were the struggles of a couple wanting to adhere to the message and making the decisions this required. There were many questions during those days and not all were answered.

During the early years, Greg and Suzanna enjoyed Andy Griffith episodes and old movies. I saw no need for either. This stance caused them to chide me as I retired to my room while the three adults watched these shows. Eventually, watching television fell by the wayside the closer we became entrenched in the new doctrines and practices coming from Spindale.

One December while at Governor's Square, we were treated to an impromptu visit from Jane and Sam Whaley. Each remarked how they loved our Christmas tree and asked us where we bought it. Greg told them. He and Suzanna beamed with pride as their tree now had Jane's approval. As far as I know, this event was never repeated. In the years following, Jane decided Christmas celebrations were not of God and they were not a part of life in WOFF.

The remaining years for Grace and Truth on Batesville Road included several memorable services. WOFF members came to help us in our prayer times. Leadership from WOFF led prayer groups and helped us "get our deliverance." The sweat rolled down our foreheads and the demons came out. Many paper towels and dishpans were used to catch the drippings and throwings. We learned God's ways and this seemed the supernatural thing to do. It got really hot in that small building, but we didn't care. We were getting free.

A couple of years after we arrived, the church moved into a large home on five acres on Blacks Drive. The church purchased the property knowing it needed many repairs and updates. This property had a large in-ground swimming pool, which proved well suited for church activities. It also had an old cemetery. In years past, the land served as home to a Baptist church. We heard the inspirational story of the church leader planting churches using this property as home base.

After moving to Blacks Drive, the service times changed to include a fellowship on Tuesday nights and a mid-week service on Thursdays. Tuesdays evolved into a time for acquaintances or relatives to join us for covered dish suppers with children playing and adults talking. We did not call them pot luck dinners since we did not believe in luck. We didn't eat deviled eggs, as no devil needed to go in, they must come out. We ate stuffed eggs. We didn't eat devil's food cake. We ate chocolate cake.

There was a whole new language to learn that increased with each minister's conference in Spindale. The new language made us feel special. We took a sense of accomplishment in learning the way God's people talk, the special speak. Take hold. You are manifesting. Have you heard God about that? You need to pull up. Open your heart. Help me, Jesus. Did you check that out? Are you locked-in? All of these phrases took on special meaning.

We learned the names of devils who we were told were in us, surrounding us, following us, assigned to us, or attacking our cars or must be too many to name. All of this added to the specialness of being among God's people who were learning God's ways. We wanted to live holy and righteous before Him in a world full of—well, you got it—devils.

We did not see the new language as a separation but felt it unified us as a group. I see now this new language allowed us to harbor an elitist attitude. We may have seen ourselves as different and special compared to other folks in Greenville or our unlearned relatives, but we did not walk in the holy heights as those from Spindale. After all, they were laying down their lives to serve God every day. We were not there.

Many of us lived in idolatry of WOFF members. We visited during special meetings and only saw the shiny side of WOFF life. Not until we were there every day and experienced what went on behind closed doors did we learn the true inner workings of that place. I now know that in the early days, they put up a front for us to see only the good things and hear the good reports. We were regarded as guests. Not until years later were we exposed to how things truly worked.

As God's ways were explained, we did not merge and compare the new practices into a context or overall reality. The lasting effects were not considered. Why? I did not know to do that. Unspoken trust in Gerald and Linda required less scrutiny of the new ways of living. I wanted to believe these new revelations were true because I wanted to belong. After all, the people around me were so loving and kind and willing to help you do anything. We stood awed by their willingness to be so helpful. Why were they being this way? I never stopped to consider that question; I enjoyed it. I wanted to be a part of it. I wanted to be as special as they appeared to be.

In 1994, we were expecting our second child. That meant we needed another place to live. We attended a meeting at the church house to discuss the "will of God" for this decision. Gerald and Linda decided we should move in with Ida Stamey**. Her house was located about fifteen minutes from the church and had plenty of room. After some instruction concerning living arrangements, paying rent and groceries, the matter was settled. We moved in January 1995. Our child was due in March.

Ida's home at 606 Central Ave was a spacious brick ranch. This property included a terraced back yard which had space for a garden. I enjoyed gardening and spending time with the children. We played in the winter snow and flew kites in the spring in a nearby field. We enjoyed working jigsaw puzzles and other family activities. The dining room was changed into a bedroom for our son born on a memorable March 13, 1995.

We were excited about our new arrival, Michael. The excitement tempered our angst over the brewing *Inside Edition* investigation into WOFF. In the hospital room on March 13th, we watched the local news channel airing a video of our pastors. The video showed the Southerlands standing near the edge of the church property, in bewilderment over the possibility that they were being filmed. Gerald and Linda were in the room with us during the news report. Though the situation was awkward, we were convinced our pastors had done no wrong. We trusted them and were happy for the support during the birth of our son. They offered few comments, but they were on the phone a great deal, walking over to the far side of the room or out in the hallway for privacy.

A few months earlier, the *Trinity Foundation* out of Dallas, TX sent Paul Eder* undercover into the Word of Faith Fellowship. He had a hidden camera and filmed many deliverance sessions and other church meetings. The tapes were released to *Inside Edition,* where Bill O'Reilly worked as host. These videos started a chain of events that did not end for many years. The Rutherford County Department of Social Services (RCDSS) was called in after other government agencies investigated. Many in the Greenville church were not provided inside knowledge of the investigation or the results. As with other WOFF dramas, information was dispensed on a need-to-know basis.

Before 1995, Word of Faith weathered other questions and accusations. Jane averted much of the damage and, by all accounts, survived those storms losing only a few members. After the new investigations addressed the questions raised from Eder's videos, they found nothing illegal, although they published information on strange practices.

Later, complaints of child abuse were registered with the RCDSS. Investigators performed assessments and took students from the school interrogating them in county-owned vehicles without a parent or a lawyer present. The investigator's questions surrounded different subjects including the child's access to television, radio, movies, sports and holidays. The series of events were later settled in June of 2005, in the outcome a case WOFF brought against RCDSS.

The months after Michael's birth were both joyous and tumultu-ous. Fears of DSS arriving to take children away started in Spindale and filtered down to us in Greenville. In South Carolina, the crisis dis-sipated and no action was taken. The investigation in North Carolina proved lengthy, invasive and poorly handled at the local level.

The name of the Greenville group changed from Grace and Truth Fellowship to Word of Life Church, Inc. We were told the change met IRS regulations. For the most part, the members of Word of Life Church were visitors to the WOFF drama on a weekly basis. We heard their version of the unfolding events. We believed it all and were be-hind the group in Spindale one hundred percent in their attempts to protect their "religious freedoms."

I later learned the irony of the whole scenario. The longer you lived inside, the less number of freedoms you enjoyed. In a bizarre twist, many of the legal battles hinged on protecting what members actually did not have—real personal freedoms. Freedoms which other Americans considered as guaranteed, normal and a part of citizenship.

CHAPTER SEVEN

THE BEST OF TIMES

While living in Mauldin, SC in 1995, we made adjustments and experienced the newfound joys of having two children. The narrative of this book describes events in my life which may seem unusual to some. In that context, I know we lived a non-normal and unusual life; however, we did have endearing moments. We were a truly loving family inside that framework. Our relationships were not predicated on the necessity of believing one certain leader as the only source of truth. That dynamic gradually changed once we moved to Spindale in 2002. But, for the years prior, we experienced good times, loving times and made memories that will last forever.

With the events set on course in 1995, the emotional losses of members increased exponentially. The number of Word of Life members in Greenville declined until the dissolving of the church in September 2002. Occasionally, a relative of a present member visited or attended Tuesday night fellowships. A couple of inmates came out of the prison ministry and visited the church. They did not stay as the loud prayer and living arrangements proved too strange. They were leaving communal living and wanted no part of it.

I did my efforts to recruit. For a while, a lady from my job attended and brought her son. The loud prayer scared the little boy, but he liked playing with the children. My sister came to visit for one service and still mentions it to this day. My parents came to our house but not to the church. I believe the oddities were too much for them. Who can blame them? Communal living, church in a basement, loud prayer, casting out devils and the ever-growing list of prohibited acts. As much as my parents loved me and my family, accepting our lifestyle, replete with these conditions, was too much for them.

As the founding pastors of Word of Life, Gerald and Linda lived in the church house along with two other families. The sanctuary, church office and a kitchen were in the basement with a large garage. The main floor, occupied by Gerald and Linda, included a large kitchen and dining room, a living room, a sitting room, a large foyer, a half bathroom and a master bedroom and large bath. There were four bedrooms on the top floor and at least one bathroom and walk-in attic space. The house was kept clean and neat.

In a passionate moment during a meeting led by WOFF ministers, Brooke Covington exclaimed, "You will grow to love this basement."

I can't say that happened for me. The basement leaked during heavy rainstorms. No, I did not learn to love that basement.

The relationships which grew during those years outweighed the meager surroundings. I enjoyed a relationship with two young men, African American twin brothers, in the church. I helped them with transportation to and from appointments and was their "guard" which included escorting them to legal appointments, doctor appointments and attending family gatherings. Accompanying them to family functions drew inquisitive looks from their relatives. All of them were friendly, but it was evident they considered my presence an odd social event. I considered this the price to pay for being in the will of God. Makes sense, right? In turn, they helped me with my work on the weekends and other tasks. We spent a lot of time together, helping each other when it was time to move or with home repairs, cleaning and other activities.

Church life in Greenville included creative fundraising. We sold greeting cards, fruit and calendars. For a while, on Tuesday nights, we paid to eat the food we brought. When we moved to WOFF, we learned we did not truly know fund-raising. Many things were that way. You could count on it. At WOFF, they were in the lead position; when they began something new, eventually we in Greenville would be guided in that direction. These new directions might include new teaching or preaching, new activities or rules and lifestyle changes.

If a new devil appeared in Spindale, by association, we had them, too. With each seminar we attended, there were more and more rules, revelations and new terms added to learn how to accurately say what God wanted us to say and how we were to live. Jane Whaley took time to explain a term and how it was used. New rules included how to clean your house, how to treat your children or your spouse, and how to treat our relatives outside the group. We were instructed how to iron our clothes and fold our underwear. Of course, we were taught how to dress, how to buy and apply make-up and which cars to own. Jane's husband, Sam helped us buy "God's car."

The Greenville church started attending Sunday evening services in Spindale. Next, through Jane sharing God's will or direction, anyone who wanted to learn how to fellowship by the Spirit of God needed to be at the church on Friday nights. WOFF weddings, personal showers and household showers or baby showers, an occasional memorial service all provided opportunities for us to go learn from God's people. Gerald and Linda started calling Jane before the Sunday morning service to check out or "lock in" what they were hearing from God for the message. This call replaced the leadership meeting in Greenville. What could local leadership add once Jane was consulted? This new level of "locking in" started after Gerald was openly corrected in Sunday night services for not following the unspoken leading or standard known only by Jane. The phrase used was "missing God" on what he preached that morning. The meant he had not submitted his heart to know what God approved for him to preach to us in Greenville. Jane knew Gerald had missed God. That was all he needed to know. He was learning submission, right?

In the years leading up to 2002, we spent many nights traveling back and forth to Spindale for services. They held special music services until the revelation came that Christmas and all holidays were of the devil. If there is one "revelation from God" that gave us more backlashes from relatives other than loud prayer or communal living, it was stopping the holiday celebrations. Jane's reason? God showed her Christmas was a birthday celebration for Jesus. Birthdays were of the devil. By the time we moved into WOFF, we did not celebrate any holidays. Many of these celebration rituals were used for us to gather as families, staying connected through fellowship and expressions of love. These times for WOFF members were redefined.

For members, any celebration evolved around weddings, personal and household showers and graduations. Memorial services were used to bring in our families and show them our sweet side. November seminars were held during Thanksgiving. However, in keeping the rules, we did not serve turkey on Thanksgiving. You were allowed to buy them at the good price before the holiday. You did not cook them until after the day passed. That makes total sense, right? These oddities were a few of the signals we missed before the merger of the two churches.

In 1999, I took a job with a company out of Atlanta selling insurance products to Credit Unions. This work lasted only a couple of years. The one benefit from that job included the salary allowing us to buy a home in the year 2000, near the church house. The memories of living in that home are the most endearing of our time as a family. We did not live with other church members. Our children each had their own room. The house needed work, and we headed in that direction. We made plans to finish the basement for another church member to live with us. During our time in that house we invited church members in for meals in addition to visits from relatives.

In a sudden turn of events, these simple dreams and plans changed.

CHAPTER EIGHT

WHAT ARE YOU HEARING?

After a service, in January of 2002, the members were told to stay and wait in the basement. At intervals, each couple was led upstairs and directed to the living room. There, curled up in a chair, sat Jane Whaley. I remember her in pants, no shoes and her legs retracted up in the chair. She appeared sleepy, yet you could sense an aura of excitement. Others in the adjoining rooms knew Jane's purpose, but each couple being led into her presence had no idea. No overt pomp and circumstance, but it appeared as if we were being allowed into the presence of royalty. For Greenville members, having a meeting with Jane was a privilege. Why were we afforded this honor? We took our place in the room facing Jane.

After she yawned, she said, "God has been speaking to me for some time that the Greenville church has to move and be a part of the Spindale church."

This introduction appeared perfunctory, but the meaning outweighed her delivery. My thoughts raced. *Did I hear her right? God said what?*

She looked directly at Martha and me, "What are you hearing?"

The magnitude of how this night could forever change my life and the life of my family slipped out of my grasp. The idolatry blinded us to the larger picture of the life-altering consequences of this decision.

I said, "Well, I know we need the breakthroughs..."

And with that reply; those waiting in the kitchen showed their glee. We were applauded. Everyone smiled and gave us hugs of congratulation, encouraging us. We passed the test.

We were admonished not to talk about it except to each other and, for certain, don't tell the children. There were other members who Jane needed to meet with that evening, to let this out "before the timing of God could bring an attack." We nodded in agreement with big smiles. We descended the stairs to the basement, finding our children and floating home.

We were not sure when, but we were headed to Spindale.

Later, we learned of the difficult time Gerald experienced with the idea of shutting down his church and moving the Spindale. He attested to God severely dealing with him until one day his heart changed. I am sure it did not hurt the hastening of the miraculous change to know that his wife, son and daughter-in-law and granddaughter were moving even if he did not. The pressures to change or be left behind were real.

We lived in our house at 34 Blacks Drive less than two years. I enjoyed that house, especially working in the flower beds and in the yard. The fenced-in backyard had plenty of room for the children to play. Having the responsibility for that yard sparked a new level of interest for yard work. This became a point of common interest with my Dad. Talking and sharing my questions helped bridge the relationship. We lived close to the church house, close enough to see someone on their back deck. There was no equity in the home, and we had no idea what we faced trying to sell it. Instead, we were head over heels excited and oblivious to the challenge. Finally, after all of these years, we were going to live in spiritual Mecca among the Chosen.

We had driven to meetings in Spindale for more than ten years and knew every inch of the drive. We knew landmarks and gas stations and clean restrooms on each of several approved paths between our home and Word of Faith Fellowship. It was exactly 59 miles from our home on Blacks Drive to the parking lot at the church by taking I-85 to Hwy 221 North. Countless were the miles driven, the gallons of gas purchased and number of snacks eaten between Greenville and Spindale during those years. Of course, the thought of not having to do all the driving was one of the first plusses considered when talking about moving to God's country.

How did we answer the questions from relatives and friends? The same way we handled other odd happenings surrounding our church, we gave them a short sound byte answer and discounted their concerns. After all they were not in the move of God. We were moving up to the place where God visits. Who knew where this could lead? This move may allow us to be "in the ministry."

We came close a few times to "one day" becoming pastors of a church in Spartanburg under Gerald and Linda. By not doing so, we averted a certain fiasco.

Upon our arrival at Grace and Truth Fellowship, Gerald and Linda shared their vision with us. They were an apostolic ministry with visions of starting a church in every county that touched Greenville County. Maps were drawn up and plans made. We learned the names of each county. We became excited when meeting someone from a chosen county-- this may be the person God uses to begin a church. My wife and I were in conversations that one day God may use us in Spartanburg. After all, I worked at a Credit Union in Spartanburg. There was a member of the church in Greenville living in Spartanburg. It made sense to start in their house and see what God would do. This vision never got off the ground. It faded into the long-forgotten, never-spoken-of dreams and wishes of pastors who get drawn into someone else's vision.

The long-time member of Grace and Truth who lived in Spartanburg eventually moved to Greenville near the church house. All the while the number of meetings Gerald and Linda attended in Spindale grew in number and they became increasingly drawn into Jane's world until one day Gerald was forced to make a choice. He chose his family and being a part of WOFF. I did not know then how the choices he made were certain to affect so many others. Who could have foreseen that?

Not every family moved from Greenville to Spindale. Naturally, the decision to stay became viewed as a sign of not being spiritual enough to hear God say "move." I regret ever having those thoughts and should have realized that not moving meant only that a few chose not to uproot and move. Those who moved thought they were moving into the will and the move of God. I could not foresee the total change in lifestyle and family dynamics that this one decision was certain to create.

Our house did not sell until September of 2003. We took over $3,000 to the closing table in order to pay off our loan, pay the realtor and other closing costs. The afternoon of the closing, the relief from being rid of the loan debt was memorable. Now, I wonder if we gave up a good place to continue living.

CHAPTER NINE

THIS IS THE WILL OF GOD?

O ur moving day was set, October 5th. Again, another big yellow truck was backed up to our door. A team of folks came to help us, and we were off to Spindale. The excitement was so thick you could taste it! After ten years, we were moving up and into the will of God.

Well, nothing ever goes perfectly in a move, right?

The house we moved into included an unfinished full basement. After we unloaded our furniture and boxes, it was truly full.

We knew the family we moved in with since our first meeting in Greenville. He was the financial-aid director at the local community college. His wife found work at the restaurant owned by a WOFF member. They had a young son. Very quickly, we found out this young boy had socialization issues. In WOFF-lingo, he had major devils. We had a glimpse of his behavioral drama in Greenville, but we were too caught up in the excitement to believe it to be an issue.

Even after this many years, words escape me to accurately describe the deep sense of astonishment and regret I soon experienced after moving into that house. The next few weeks contained the biggest test of my faith in WOFF to that point. What had we done? A member from Greenville found out we moved into that house. "Oh, you're moving in there?" She lived with this family for several years in Greenville and smiled with glee that she now lived elsewhere.

In the midst of all the other adjustments to make, we did not need these issues, too. But, face them we did. The fact that Gerald and Linda knew the raging drama this family lived in, angered and confused me. They allowed us to move in there. The results told me the Southerlands were not in charge of anything. They were mere marionettes on Jane's strings very early in the transition. I felt stuck. Making two house payments was not a viable option. My wife and I moved into the room over the garage. We stayed there for six years. The daily drama bordered on depressing, and no one admitted to believing in depression at WOFF. As each month passed, I longed for a way to move my family out of that house.

In this new household, as with others, we split the cost of groceries and shared the kitchen. When one person cooked the meal, the others washed the dishes. Many nights we rotated the cooking duties. At other times, we ate as separate families. Frequently, we ate our meals separated from the other family. I now believe their son wanted some personalized attention and did not know how to ask for it without showing out. The events he instigated included acts of direct defiance to the known behavioral norms. He would hit or taunt our children as well as talk about subjects not approved, asking socially awkward questions at just the right moment to get a reaction. He also broke the established house rules for bathroom behaviors and cleanliness. During my time in this house, he did not get what he needed to mature and stabilize. He received daily spankings, sometimes more than once a day. He hollered and screamed and put a funk on the whole house.

Most Sundays, we tried to eat dinner with the other family. For months and then years, at meal time, this young boy did something to aggravate or instigate some obvious drama, laughing the whole time. As a result, he was taken upstairs to the parent's room for his "correction." The correction could include loud prayer or spankings or both. We did our best to ignore the drama, but it went past sad right to unmanageable and ludicrous. Weeks upon weeks, months upon months, year after year; the father or mother "disciplined" this child. Now, I believe he needed the professional counseling that the church did not believe in. The stark irony? Help for him was closer than we all realized.

The first few weeks of being inside WOFF were spent getting the lay of the land. I worked a few days a week in Greenville for a Credit Union. Soon, I found another part-time job at a Credit Union in Marion, thirty minutes north of Spindale. After a service, I was called into Jane's office.

In the office were several members of leadership hovering and watching. They may not have been listening, but I remember the setting as a court or council.

Jane spoke, "This is Josh Farmer. He needs someone to work part-time. It may turn into full time later. He is not sure, yet. You would be working for him painting and helping get apartments ready. If you feel that this is your job, let him know. Carry it, pray about it"

At that moment, I did not know enough to ask questions nor did there appear to be a door for them. Josh stood off to her side with his hands in his pockets glancing my way attempting to read my reaction. After a nod in his direction, I was told to let him know what I was "hearing" in the next few days.

And with that meeting, I started a relationship with Josh Farmer, his father Ray Farmer and Two Mile Properties, LLC. I took the job in December of 2002. My time working for the Farmers included many ups and downs until my exit in 2008. During the first meeting, the prospect of working with other church members excited me. Though I lived in daily household drama, this job sounded like it may help me to get further into the will of God.

PART TWO

LIFE INSIDE WOFF

CHAPTER TEN

SIGNATURE PRACTICE OF LOUD PRAYER, BLASTING AND DELIVERANCE

WOFF in Spindale contained about 450 members composed of many smaller groups with ever-changing components. In an earlier chapter, I have briefly described the unique prayer but will give more details in this chapter. Next, I will review the practices surrounding money, including fundraisers. After this, I will review a few of the pivotal services which changed our lives as members, including the practice of not celebrating holidays. This section will end with a narrative concerning the many rules inside this group and a schedule for a typical week.

The loud prayer is the most evident signature practice for WOFF. Jane used it as the central theme of our stance to defend our religious freedom. My involvement in this prayer numbers in the thousands of sessions. I participated in WOFF culture and practices from mid-February of 1992 until July 10, 2008. This totals nearly 6,000 days. For many weeks in Greenville and later inside WOFF, there was prayer at the church six days a week. That equals about 300 days during a calendar year. During the earlier seminars, prayer occurred three times a day. In later years, the sessions were less numerous, but none the less intense. What I describe here stems from intimate and frequent participation. Who can deny my experience with this definitive practice? I do not practice loud prayer or deliverance now, nor do I know of any ex-WOFF members that do. One ex-member expressed to me his hesitation in telling others that he participated in this kind of prayer because he did not feel comfortable in answering the questions it provoked. I welcome the questions; I understand how and why I participated and how it affected my life.

As mentioned, my first experience with loud prayer occurred in the second service at the Greenville church. Upon arriving, we heard the drums and loud noise while in the parking lot. Shrugging off any doubts or questions, we went in and encountered a prayer service like none other. Afterwards, I voiced my questions. Answers were given. Many years have passed; I do not remember all of the questions, but a few scriptures provided during that time stuck with me.

*"But if I drive out the demons by the **finger** of **God**, then the kingdom of God has [already] come upon you."* (Amplified © Bible Luke 11:20)

This one was given to explain the use of the hands in the air. Yes, I think we were pointing to the devils and telling them to go.

*"After the Lord has washed away the [moral] filth of the daughters of Zion [pride, vanity, haughtiness] and has purged the bloodstains of Jerusalem from the midst of it by the spirit and **blast** of judgment and by the spirit and **blast** of burning and sifting."* (Isaiah 4:4 AMP)

This reference was used to explain and justify the forceful "blasting" term, thus the loudness and angry expressions on our faces. The person's anger was directed toward the devil(s).

*Hear, oh, hear the **roar** of His voice and the sound of rumbling that goes out of His mouth!* (Job 37.2 AMP)

This reference was used to explain the loudness and the forcefulness. The Hebrew word for "roar" was explained as a "high shrill sound."

Considering these Scriptures, does the loud prayer activity make sense? These scriptures and more were used to verify or validate the loud sounds and pointing of the fingers that were exhibited while praying. Several other scriptures with the word "blast" or "deliverance" and others about the loud sounds of God were used as justification for this practice. Because of my background in the Word movement and my desire for help, I accepted these Scriptures as validation that what was being practiced was from God. I placed trust in the leadership, so I trusted their answers. When others around you were gleefully showing their interest and need for this prayer, you quickly recognized the cues that to refuse meant rejected membership in the group.

Michael Cuneo wrote *American Exorcism: Expelling Demons in the Land of Plenty* [2] and dedicated a chapter titled "Carolina Blues" to his visit to Spindale. He shared his impressions of WOFF members and their leader. He attempted to experience this practice of prayer first hand. Though he was allowed to attend a service, the denial of his request serves as an announcement to others that this practice remains sacred to the faithful members.

My desire here is not to impugn or attack other members who participated alongside me in these activities. I do not assess the sincerity or insincerity of others as I share my personal reflections. By sharing my perspective, I desire to answer the questions of many who have never been a part of loud prayer or deliverance. If I censor the details and keep the methods used secret, I do a huge disservice to my readers. How can it be reasoned that a religious group containing secret activities be allowed to hide those practices from the very public which they are attempting to recruit? How can there be WOFF secrets when their efforts in the media over the last few years have been to convince all that they are a safe group with "nothing to hide?"

WOFF receives more public scrutiny because of loud prayer, blasting and deliverance than any other activity to this point. As mentioned, an undercover investigation launched by the Trinity Foundation included a new member filming the prayer sessions and releasing them to *Inside Edition* in February of 1995. Bill O'Reilly was the anchor at that time. The segment received a great amount of attention and served as the spring board for the local and state authorities to launch investigations into the activities of the church. The link to O'Reilly's report is here.

(https://www.youtube.com/watch?v=YwE5fBT9RYE)[3]

Through a long, involved sequence of events, law suits and custody battles, the culmination of this public drama occurred in a civil suit filed in 2003, pitting WOFF against the local Rutherford County Department of Social Services (RCDSS). (WOF vs. RCDSS, Civil Action 1:03CV298)[4] This lawsuit produced a compromise now commonly known as the "federal injunction." In the case, Judge Lacy Thornburg, Jr. awarded attorney fees of $300,000 to be paid by RCDSS to WOFF. This compromise might have been well intended; however, the resulting fears and subsequent negligence of the legally mandated duties of RCDSS to quickly investigate and protect the children of WOFF have caused many to wonder if RCDSS will ever again properly do their job. In my opinion, the results prove that the "Cure has become the disease" in this case.

The term "blasting" was frequently used to describe the prayer including the "shrill sounds." These sounds emanated from pushing the diaphragm upwards and included accompanying hand motions. Using the upper throat to make these sounds damages the vocal chords. After prayer sessions, folks sounded hoarse. Halls® cough drops were recommended and sometimes passed out to members for relief. The "shrills sounds" were similar to a high-pitched screaming but could, also, include lower tones depending on the person praying. The hand motions are best described as a purposed raising of the hand open or closed in a fist extending in a forward and upward motion. The loudest person I ever heard "pray," no doubt, was Jane Whaley. A blasting session may be over a person or a group of people or include a group of members praying to "hit the heavens" in order to cause a certain effect. One instance I recall involved the congregation praying that Josh Farmer could sell one of his repossessed jets to a person in Dubai. This prayer included the sale and Josh, in turn, donated a good part of the proceeds to the church.

Sometimes, we also prayed as a group to "hit the heavens" for no particular outcome only the "will of God" in a situation.

During the years of outside examination and media scrutiny, substituting the term "loud prayer" for "blasting" became acceptable. There appeared to be less baggage associated with the term. In WOFF, "blasting" and "loud prayer" meant the same thing.

Blasting and loud prayer often went hand in hand with someone getting "deliverance." This could include one person praying alone, but many times other members helped them "get their deliverance."

The quickest way to see what deliverance looks like is to watch the *Inside Edition* video. These sessions included more than blasting. Most often, the person receiving the prayer sat in the middle of the group where others could touch and lay hands on them, usually on the upper back or neck area. I have been a part of prayer groups where the leader put a hand on the subject's stomach and pushed while talking or praying near the person's ear. The leader of the group may take a position sitting close to the person in the middle. Usually, men prayed for men and boys, and women prayed for women and girls. Young people and children followed this same guideline. However, there were always exceptions to the rules, "as God leads" and Jane approves.

When prayer and deliverance sessions occurred in the sanctuary, it began with the congregation rearranging the chairs into circles of varying sizes. Members of leadership perched on the platform to oversee the process. They guided which members went into each group. The right members were sent to your group to help you get a "breakthrough." As the chairs were being arranged, buckets or dish pans and paper towels were retrieved from the closet at the right side of the platform. Someone in the group took the time to pre-tear paper towels and hand them to you to hold on your lap for future use. In later years, the dishpans were omitted. The used paper towels were piled by your chair and picked up at the end of the deliverance service. If you ran out of paper towels, a member scurried to the restrooms to grab a roll of toilet paper. Toilet paper did not help when someone vomited.

Once the groups were set, the word was given the word from leadership to get started. As with the growing roar of an airplane engine, the noise level inside those four walls increased. Once it reached the maximum pitch, the high volume required you to be very close to anyone to hear them. Conversations were held leaning up into the person's head to get close to their ear. I don't remember the exact time during my tour when, Dr. Pagter from the group told me to wear ear plugs during prayer. I already had a hearing loss, and he felt that exposing me to prayer without protection would worsen the loss. Initially, I became embarrassed to wear the plugs and sometimes forgot them. For those times, I stuffed paper towels or toilet tissue into my ears. Even with the ear plugs, I heard the talking because of the high volume of the speakers. After I started wearing the ear plugs, I noticed others using them during prayer and more parents covering the infant's ears.

Yes, everyone participated in these prayer times. Children and senior citizens were not exempt. Should we have been concerned about constant exposure to that level of noise? Many times the loud group prayer extended for two or more hours. I experienced hearing delays after many prayer sessions similar to the feeling at the airport after being too close to a plane taking off.

During the first few months of participating in loud prayer, I saw folks become flushed in the face from bending over for extended periods of time. Small red blotches appeared on their faces. There was air conditioning, but that did not matter, you were fighting devils and sweat showed you were in the fight.

If you were the one receiving prayer, you bent over in a chair while others prayed over you. Some folks pushed on your back to help you bend over. I never enjoyed that part because of my large belly; it hurt to bend over for any length of time. At times, I told the group leader that I must sit up to relieve the stress on my middle. I felt so unspiritual when this happened. Why?

In the sanctuary, once we got the word to start, the person getting prayer may lean over with elbows on their legs and begin saying "Help me, Jesus." You might get instructions from the group leader to begin another way. You might be told to stand up and "hit-it" and begin "blasting the heavens." No matter how, you got started and you must appear engaged. If you appeared "spaced out" or "out there in your thoughts" you were told to "take hold of your mind."

The leader of your group could ask you what sin you were giving to. Or the leader may tell you what God told them about your sin. It may be something you agree with or not, but, regardless, it took gumption to deny a leader "nailing your sin and hitting your devils." If you agreed, then things went better for you. If you disagreed, you only delayed your "deliverance" and lengthened the time "in the chair." Others in the group may or may not be told about your sin; this depended on the leader. Rest assured, by the next group meeting, that leader told someone in authority, over them or over you, if you received your deliverance. That person might have told Jane.

Some of these sessions lasted for hours, some for three hours or more. In many of those meetings, we all sweated profusely and, yet, counted it as glory, smiling at each other in the glow of an unspoken common devotion to the cause—getting devils out.

There were some odd manifestations during group prayer. It was not unusual to see forty or fifty men or youth standing on the platform and praying and "hitting the heavens." When participating in this kind of prayer, it was helpful if others around you were doing the same thing. During prayer you could see people lying in the aisles or all over the platform crying out to God for a breakthrough, weeping and helping others to get a breakthrough. This prayer time might go on for an extended time.

The oddest manifestation of group behavior during prayer is an occurrence I call "prayer scrums." Women and girls usually did not exhibit this behavior, but the men and boys did. A person getting prayer in the middle of a large group may be laying or kneeling on the floor. Maybe gradually, or sometimes suddenly, a large group of people piled themselves on top of that person and each other, all the while continuing the noises associated with loud prayer and deliverance. This looks dangerous to the untrained or new member.

Over the years, I witnessed many of these scrums. I never heard any reasoning for this behavior, and no one commented on the form of it. The only expressions passed to each other were smiles when the person got their "breakthrough." There was satisfaction knowing you had been a part of it. Afterwards, everyone looked like they had participated in a wrestling match... tucking in their shirts and wiping up their sweat.

As the years passed and for no obvious reason, the longer prayer sessions grew more infrequent, but no less intense. Seminars changed from three meetings a day to two. We were told to get the children home and get them some rest. Adults may get some rest, too. There were other places where you could get the deliverance you so desperately needed.

Allow me to continue.

As a faithful member, you were always expected to want deliverance; you might be called off of your job and told to come to the church to get prayer. If you refused, you better have a good reason, or you were disciplined or scolded for not wanting prayer. Admonishments included: What devil are you giving to? Open your heart and tell the sin you gave to.

If you worked at a member-owned company, you could get prayer at your job with your co-workers praying. This happened if you were "under it" or "giving to a devil."

Your need for prayer and deliverance might be met in your household. You may have been attacked by an "unclean devil" in your dreams and needed to be freed in order to get back to what little sleep you could get before the sun came up. Your family or other household members might be awakened at 3AM to help you get a breakthrough. And their attitudes better be good about praying at 3AM or they may be next.

Every member was expected to want loud prayer and deliverance. Members were expected to show eagerness about getting free from devils. You might be told you needed prayer because someone around you felt something wasn't right with you and you were under attack and did not know it. Your feelings were not important, the only concern—did you need the devil driven out of you? You did not have to agree whether you had a particular kind of devil. Your faithfulness to the mantra, to the group, to God and, of course, to Jane showed in that you agreed to receive prayer. No matter if you understood it, you wanted that devil out of you.

To the unlearned, this may all sound shocking and surreal. I guarantee that these words barely convey the all-encompassing lifestyle which awaits members. WOFF-life was truly a totally engaged experience. Once you lived in a household surrounded by members 24/7 and on your job, then your reality became their reality and vise versa. That reality was governed by how, when and what Jane heard from God about you, your family, your household, the church.

For a season, the individual deliverance groups were called truth circles. At the start of a truth circle, the leader asked the person getting prayer what had God showed them? If nothing was mentioned then the group leader might tell the others in the group to begin praying and "hitting the heavens." The person receiving prayer started to "cry out to God" or give in to the "groanings" while others "blasted the heavens." There were no written instructions or exact approved methods. We learned from watching others and informal instruction from leadership.

Many times the leader asked more questions. Depending on the answers, the group might pray a different way. Prayer continued until the person got a "breakthrough." A breakthrough was any sign of improvement, sometimes after they had coughed up stuff. Throughout the whole process, Jane Whaley and the leadership moved from group to group checking to see if there was progress. They might join in and help pray for a while or give additional instructions.

The dynamics of these groups changed over the years. Thus, it is difficult to share absolutes. Did people change or "get free?" Many times, a person received prayer for the same thing over and over.

Was this type of prayer the total answer to walking in a relationship with Jesus? No.

Did folks become confused wondering why they were unable to conquer whatever sin or behavior that required the prayer? Yes.

Those who doubted had a hard time being changed by whatever method was being used, whether this meant prayer, reading scriptures or listening to tapes. It took years for me to realize that having others pray deliverance was not the panacea that we were led to believe.

Deliverance prayer also occurred in large groups with no particular person being the central focus. Members were grouped for "deliverance" prayer aimed at a certain purpose. Children were grouped to pray against rebellion, back-talking or unclean thoughts. Adults might pray against fear of death, unclean thoughts, and perversion. If members participated in Free Masons, Eastern Star, Boy Scouts, Girl Scouts, Amway, witchcraft, karate or martial arts of any type—they were in a deliverance group for that.

What was the attraction? Why would anyone submit themselves to this deliverance?

This practice was the central defining evidence of separation between us and anyone else. We followed the mantra: "It is a privilege to receive prayer (in this manner) and a privilege to help others in prayer." If you believed the testimonies of others about the prayer, then you submitted and did what everyone else was doing. We were encouraged to be "hungry for deliverance." It was uncomfortable at first, but we learned new things from those who already knew "how to pray."

If a new member refused prayer then their time in this group was short. If a new person was not willing to "give up their devils," WOFF became a hard place to live. If you hoped to stay and flourish, then submitting to blasting prayer and deliverance was in your near future. Once, when I showed some resistance to prayer, the leader of the group took me by the shoulders and shook me back and forth while screaming: "Come out of him you stubborn devils!" This type of encouragement was a common occurrence for many, especially in the early years of WOFF. A person might be pushed back and forth and side to side as well as pushed from the back in order to help get those devils out. I know, I had it done to me, and I have helped others in that way, though never beyond their perceived agreement to the prayer.

Simply stated, blasting was the WOFF weapon of choice. The whole church may be told to "hit the heavens" for someone's healing, physical protection in the face of a threat, or finances for an individual, business, family or the church. Other prayer included Jane's court cases; child custody cases; wisdom for lawyers in the DSS case, Judge Randy Pool or whoever may be hearing a certain court case; local, state and federal elections; the President or other government leaders; law enforcement officers; trips out of town or out of the country to Brazil or Africa. Any number of things could be the subject of blasting prayer.

In times of group prayer, leaders told members to "take hold of your minds—many of you are staring off and not thinking about what you are praying for." Now, I realize this was evidence of mind control techniques.

A few times, I witnessed members reaching a point of stress and not knowing how to move past it. They might show irrational behavior or flip out. I saw members run out of the building and be chased by a group to help them "get back in their place." I witnessed one young man who ran up to the school and was surrounded by a large group of folks who allowed him no exit. He looked dazed, obviously having issues with one of the church leaders. I only saw the midpoint of this intervention, not the beginning or the end. The young man was put on discipline for several days after an intense long prayer and deliverance session back inside the church.

I am sad to say that because I was not close to this young person, I left and took no action to help him. The group was so large; it was not practical to get involved with every issue, every time. Plus, I believed the typical assumption that the person running from prayer was automatically wrong. *Who runs from prayer? Who in their right mind would not want to "get their demons out?"* Entertaining the thought that not wanting prayer could be acceptable was dangerous. To defend that notion, you believed the trite, thought-stopping phrases provided by the group. They helped you stay locked in. This reasoning worked great until you did not want prayer. You knew you were not trying to hide sin.

There were penalties for members who were not directly involved in a situation involving other members or expressed an opinion or took some action without being "locked-in." You had to choose your battles.

We, also, met for prayer at the church Monday through Friday at 11:00AM. Those without regular employment or working second shift were expected to attend. If you worked close by or for a member-owned company, it might mean you attended as part of your lunch break. Others in attendance included the elderly, students of the WOFF School who were on in-school suspension or discipline, the mildly sick, the caretakers with young babies, and church staff. There might be a hundred or more members in attendance.

For years, Gerald Southerland led this prayer service. Others in leadership filled in if Gerald was off the property or in another activity. The service began with announcements, individual prayer requests, prayer requests for those outside the church that were on a "watch list," a relative of a member or someone the church was "taking hold of." For those under attack, a group of members could gather around them and offer deliverance prayer. Many times this was without the buckets, but someone may get paper towels if they "heard in their spirit" they were needed.

Gerald stopped the session from time to time and gave instruction. "I see some of you checking out…take hold of your minds."

"Let's hit the heavens for the will of God for the businesses in the church."

"Let's blast those devils attacking the finances of God's people!"

"Now, go in that place in God to pray strong and give your whole heart for the last few minutes we have together."

"Jane is out of the country; let's carry her, guard her in the Spirit and hold her up in prayer throughout the day for God's will in that situation."

During this service, members were constantly reminded to think about church financial needs. It was an often repeated request: we need more money for the church budget.

This service lasted until noon or a little after.

After the service, members were expected to gather all the used tissues or paper towels and vacuum around the chairs and clean bathrooms. A church staff member might ask for volunteers to do projects around the church that afternoon. This was the one service where there was no offering collected.

CHAPTER ELEVEN

DID YOU SIGN THE WAIVER?

T he *Inside Edition* video, released in February 1995, set in motion events which have forever affected WOFF members,
survivors and their families. Members were information-managed
then, and the years since have proved no different. During that era,
information was filtered through the leadership structure in Spindale
and the Greenville church. I refused to independently seek out news
sources because of the drama and a fear of consequences if I was
found out. Also, I wanted to believe that the important matters were
shared with regular members. Members caught "going out from under
God's protection and reading news sources" were openly castigated,
rebuked and put on discipline. To this day, I do not know the exact
events which prompted the requirement for us to sign the Waiver and
Release. Those that know still keep it among themselves.

After leaving WOFF, a friend gave me a copy of the Waiver and
Release. I don't remember exactly when I signed this document. For
certain, my wife and I signed one. If I was given a copy, I do not
know where it is right now. If there were different versions, I am not
aware. As far as I know, the version included at the end of this book is
the version I signed.

I am not an attorney and my limited experience with contracts in-
volves ones for money owed. I, also, have limited experience with

rental contracts and lease agreements for houses and apartments. Over the years, I have signed other contracts as we all do in the course of living; however, I do not claim to be an expert on documents such as this Waiver and Release. I can only share my opinions, reflections and lots of questions.

This document specifically addressed issues surrounding the signature practice of loud prayer. We were told that some had left and "attacked" the church. We were told this Waiver protected the church from others making false claims and future attacks. Most importantly, Jane and her leaders declared, *"No one gets prayer or hands laid on them without signing the document."*

Let's put this into focus. How often did members participate in blasting prayer and deliverance? Innumerable times, service after service, more days praying than not praying. What was the attitude toward this honored and revered practice? Your salvation may depend on it. Your ability to fight the devils assigned to you was weak unless you sought loud prayer and deliverance. How long did it take for most members to decide to sign this form? You got it; no time at all. To delay was considered rebellion.

After a few months, this document and the mention of it faded into the lost annals of WOFF history. If it is used any longer, I do not know. However, I doubt if the signed copies have been destroyed. This document came along before WOFF financed, supported and acquired their in-house legal counsel.

The issue of this waiver was introduced before a seminar in late 1995 or early 1996. I remember we were still commuting from Greenville. We were required to sign this document before or after a Sunday evening service. Tables and chairs were in the foyer of the sanctuary or in the fellowship hall, and members, serving as NC notaries, sat behind the tables with copies of the waiver. As you stepped up, you were given a copy and allowed to "read" it.

The scene looked real official. It was a foregone conclusion that anyone "walking with God" and who wanted "God's will in their life" would sign the waiver. Anyone who was "submitted to Jesus" wanted "deliverance from devils in them." This document was the ticket for you continuing to get what you claimed had helped you: loud prayer, blasting and deliverance. You knew that "only those in rebellion and defiant against God" refused prayer.

Though I did not recognize the strength of it, the social pressure to conform and "be a part of the move of God" was intense. To a faithful member's perspective, this was the opportunity to bask in the privilege of being asked to sign and, thus, stay in the move of God. Life in this subculture included several situations requiring decisions within the confines of intense religious-based social pressure. This was the norm involving decisions about behaviors, money, and the use of specific terms. Everyone else was doing it, why hold back? Are you giving to that "independent spirit?"

The question remains: "John, how could you sign this document and give your rights away?"

The truth is I had no idea I was *waiving* or *releasing* Jane Whaley, Sam Whaley or other WOFF leadership from anything. I believed, regardless of the words on the page, we were *gaining something*, not losing anything. We were gaining prayer, deliverance, and freedom from devils. Yes, that is the best explanation I can give.

Was I actually able to think clearly about this document at that time? From Steven Hassan's book, *Combatting Cult Mind Control.*[5] *"When I lecture in colleges, I usually challenge my audience with the question, "How would you **know** if you were under mind control?" After some reflection, most people will realize that if one were under mind control, it would be impossible to determine it without some help from others. In addition, **one would need to understand very clearly what mind control is.**" (Page 53 emphasis added).*

While inside WOFF, it was impossible to have known that I was under mind control. The pressures and dynamics surrounding the signing of this waiver were not explained to members. I will come back to this point as we review the document itself.

Did I read the document before I signed it? What do you think? I don't remember reading it in detail; I probably glanced over it. But, I had signed it in my mind before I signed it at the table. Dangerous? At the least, it was not prudent. When I first reread this Waiver after leaving WOFF, I exploded. How could I have been so duped? The simplest explanation? I was under mind control. I wonder if other former members remember their thoughts when signing the Waiver. What were they thinking when they gave the notary a dollar and then they gave it back? Consideration must be exchanged for the agreement or contract to be legal. Now, the whole scene shines as an example of religious junk.

The first part of the waiver states the basics. We filled in our name. I am not sure what was put in the blank titled City. The church property is not in the Spindale city limits. So, what did we put there? Next, the one dollar is explained. The notaries did not keep the dollar. It was always returned to the person signing. Next, there is more about the legality of WOFF.

Item Number 2 describes the content of church services. Members and participants, *"taking part in the worship services at said church, do speak in tongues, do have deliverance, do have healing services, do have casting out of devils services and in most of the usual and normal services as are carried on in charismatic evangelical services:."* If this statement was meant to cast WOFF as a normal, charismatic, evangelical church, I believe the facts speak differently. Do the majority of other charismatic evangelical churches in this country have the same practices as we did? And what other churches require Waivers before ministering to members or visitors?

Next is the disclaimer of warranty (#3). There are NO guarantees with what WOFF offers. They did not guarantee you will be healed, delivered from devils, and they gave no guarantee your soul will be saved or that your mental and/or emotional condition will be cured. Also, *"...that the parties of the second part do not hold out that they have any education nor practice whatsoever in psychiatry, psycholo-*

gy, mental counseling, marital counseling, nor are they experts in any field whatsoever that might have to do with the spirit or the physical thing of a person, except that which is taught in the Word of God; they make no claim whatsoever, should a person receive healing, deliverance, spirit filling or any other condition that they will not digress from this condition and return to their old condition;

That all the healings, casting out of demons and deliverance are done through prayer and ministry of the Word of God."

I don't believe anyone at WOFF was an expert at anything. This has changed over the years. Now, they have members in dentistry, several doctors and at least one nurse with a concentration in psychiatric care. There are other nurses and at least one Family Nurse Practitioner. Do they practice on church property? Yes. I had more than one examination by a doctor at the church. I was given more than one prescription by a doctor while there. My children received at least preliminary examinations at the church. I thought nothing of it but considered it part of the all-encompassing lifestyle of the church.

The waiver contains language stating what the member is requesting: *"the blessing that God may have for me through the prayer and ministry of the Word of God, be it through deliverance, healing, casting out demons or **anything else** which might happen to me during the ministry at Word of Faith Fellowship..."*(Emphasis added.)

Anything else? This statement includes, well, anything.
The document continues to list what a member was waiving. Can anyone definitively waive their *rights,* either present or future, especially, if the rights arise from future actions of the second party: WOFF, Jane, Sam and those who act on behalf of WOFF? I am not sure, but, in my opinion this is the weakest part of the entire document.

In retrospect, I did not hear a peep about this document for the last few years of my time with WOFF. After a while, new members were not publicly required to sign them. This may have happened in an office somewhere. Is the copy I signed still valid? If Jane received counsel and considered this a valid document in the past, are there now any parts she still considers operational and protecting her and other ministers? I have no knowledge that the validity of this document was ever tested in court.

The member signing, also, waived the right to recover monetary damages for any number of various occurrences. *"I waive my right of any action for monetary damages resulting from so called spiritual, mental, financial, emotional, physical, social, or loss, suffered as a result of any ministry given to me by any person associated directly and indirectly with the Word of Faith Fellowship, Inc., including ministry received by me from any visitors."*

I cannot believe I signed this document

It never occurred to me I would be injured from my involvement in blasting prayer specifically or WOFF-life in general.

When I re-read the waiver after leaving WOFF, the next part captured my attention: *"I understand that in some spiritual atmospheres there may be some mind control involved, however, after witnessing the ministry and atmosphere of Word of Faith Fellowship, Inc., I believe that the pastors and other persons connected with The Word of Faith Fellowship, Inc. do not operate in mind control, they operate in the power and anointing of God."*

Let's go through this again.

While unknowingly UNDER mind control we were told in order to continue receiving the signature practice and benefit and service of WOFF we had to attest *"...that the pastors and other persons connected with The Word of Faith Fellowship, Inc. do not operate in mind control..."*

Who among us actually knew what mind control was when we signed that paper? I did not.

How could those under mind control explain to those under mind control that they were all not under mind control? To quote Jane Whaley, "When you are deceived, you are deceived." She always referenced others' deceptions with that comment.

*"I have discussed this document with the Reverend Sam G. Whaley, Jr. and/or Reverend Jane B. Whaley or an employee of The Word of Faith Fellowship, Inc. and they have explained to me, **in detail, what is going to take place.** I have been advised by the Reverends Whaley and/or other agents of the Word of Faith Fellowship, Inc. that it is my duty, if I do not understand this document, to take it to a lawyer of my choice, before executing this Agreement."*

Yes. I signed this agreement without taking it to an attorney. I had no understanding that this event was a *buyer beware* situation. After all those signing this document beside me at the table were my friends. Why consider this a bad thing? It was in reality, buyer be pressured, buyer be fooled.

Did anyone ever get a detailed explanation of what waited for them after they joined WOFF and before signing this or before actually joining WOFF? Did anyone from WOFF explain to anyone before they signed this document why WOFF felt it was necessary to state its ministers did not practice mind control?

This next statement sums up the matter for me. *"I fully understand this Agreement and what it means. This Agreement is made with my full knowledge of its content and (I) am fully aware of the danger that arises out of any mental or spiritual exorcism."*

Who knew the *"danger that arises out of any mental or spiritual exorcism"* if no one administering the exorcism claimed to be trained or educated in *"...nor practice(d) whatsoever in psychiatry, psychology, mental counseling, marital counseling, ... "*? How could a regular member signing this document know what they were getting into when they were so under the spell of the leader? I have asked myself how I signed it and can only explain I was under the same mind control that the document itself denied.

Does that make sense? It does to me now. This entire scene, prompted by who knows what, stands as a proclamation to the extensive chicanery the leaders of WOFF were able to enact on the faithful members.

CHAPTER TWELVE

PRACTICES CONCERNING MONEY

Many times we prayed for breakthroughs targeted at bringing in money for the church. The stage filled up with members leading others to give their "whole heart to the prayer." For hours, we blasted "the heavens for the devil to let go of God's blessings for His people." The evidence of answered, successful prayer meant those blessings ended up in the church coffers. If this happened, then the prayer was deemed to have worked. Simple, right?

While inside this group, I did not see the practices concerning money as a complete distraction from more important matters. I did not believe I could influence the handling of the money. No one asked my opinion. The personal finances of our family were a different matter. I struggled in this area to earn enough money to just get through the week. I focused on being able to pay our bills and provide for my family. When you are in the throes of such an evolving, dynamic subculture, you pick your battles. That is not to say I did not complain and try to earn more money. I certainly did.

In the late summer of 2003, I took action that landed me in trouble. At that time, I worked for Two Mile Properties at Creekside Apartments in Gaffney, SC. My duties as manager included purchasing the cleaning chemicals. The chemical salesman mentioned they were looking for representatives. This sparked my interest since I was quite impressed with the chemicals. I called for an interview and a couple days later, I met with the regional manager at a hotel in Gaffney. After leaving the interview, I knew I did not want the job, but considering other possibilities for income gave me hope. I casually mentioned the interview to my wife.

At the next church service I felt a tap on my shoulder from behind. One of our leaders stood behind me. "Come outside."

There in the grass by the steps in front of the church stood a few church leaders. As I approached this group, my thoughts raced. *What had I done?*

Ray Farmer began, "I heard about the job interview. The interview was not gotten ahold of in God."

Two other leadership folks stood listening. One of them owned another construction company.

Karel Reynolds approached coming down the sidewalk on the side of the sanctuary. "I just got off the phone with Jane in Brazil. Jane was very grieved that you would do something like this without getting ahold of this in God. We don't do things like that **out from under authority**. You need to find a place of repentance for even allowing the thought of going to that interview."

At this point, the pressures mounted up to more than I could take. I started to cry. Okay, maybe it was blubbering.

I realize now that the leadership took this as a sign of my agreement. This sign meant I was seeking a place of repentance. *That could not have been further from the truth!* The emotions gushed forth from being told to repent for not asking permission before looking for another job. Repent for even allowing the thought. The financial pressures were too great to ignore. Somewhere in the crying, I explained that the pay from Two Mile and the part-time work did not meet our financial needs.

Ray spoke up, "Is Martha getting paid for teaching in the school?"

"No."

Ray volunteered an option. "I have been carrying it that she should get paid. Let me talk to Jane about that."

This incident should have clarified in my thinking that the phrase *"getting ahold of things in God"* meant asking Jane for permission to do something. Also, *"being out from under authority"* meant you **had not** asked Jane for permission. Any delusion about how things worked should have been cleared up for me.

The result? I endured a scolding for seeking employment outside the church. I went to an interview for a job that I didn't want. Never mind the long hours I worked and the financial pressures, I had not asked permission. I had sinned by even thinking the thought, and I needed to repent.

A point that slipped past me at the time was that the other people in the meeting acted like the whole process of taking me out of the sanctuary and telling me that Jane disapproved of my actions was normal. Apparently, everyone else knew how sinful my sin was to "be out from under authority." They already knew who ran the church. I was a slow learner.

The next month in my journal, I recorded that Josh Farmer helped us with pay advances, and we received financial help from relatives. A little while after this incident, my wife started receiving a check for teaching in the school. We needed the money, and I believe my wife earned it. She spent many hours teaching and coordinating the fund raisers for the school. We were not rich; we were barely getting by.

Many rumors ran through the surrounding community about WOFF. One of them claimed church members handed their checks in and were, afterwards, given allowances. I did not hand over my check every week and then receive an allowance. We gave in the offering plates as they were passed. Those offering plates were passed almost every service. Many times, the plates were passed three or four times in one service.

The plates were passed for missions or wedding expenses or teacher salaries or church property insurance or whatever the crisis happened to be for that week. Sam exhorted everyone to "hear God the first time so we don't have to keep passing the plates."

I once heard Brooke exclaim, "Why don't you just give it all the first time?"

After passing the plates the first time, the service may go on or there may be a pause for announcements. Workers in the office counted the money. If there was not enough, a messenger hurried back to the sanctuary telling whoever stood at the podium that we needed another offering. A target figure may be announced: we need another $15,000 or $25,000.

This prompted the next prayer from Sam or another leader:

"Ok, we are going to pray. Since the church budget is not met yet, someone is not hearing God. Take a minute and inquire of God. We really need to move on to other things. God has things for us to do, and we need this taken care of before we move on. Father, we ask you tonight for a miracle offering, speak to the hearts of the people. Cause them to hear Your word and give as You see fit. You know our needs, Father. We believe You and You are our source. In Jesus' Name, Amen. Ok, serve the people." (pass the plates, again)

If I heard prayers like that once, I heard them a thousand times. Toward the end of my tour, Jane told us that she "felt led to check the offering records." She knew who tithed and who did not. She admitted to knowing if the giving changed and if the job or income had not changed. In addition, several members had their tax returns completed by tax preparers in the church. The tax preparers knew your income. If you did not tithe, they could hear God and report back to Jane that you were in sin by not tithing. You could get a rebuke or even a letter saying you were robbing God; you needed to repent and start tithing. No pressure, right?

End of the year summary statements for giving were provided to church members; however, we never were given a summary of church spending in an open meeting. Jane may have told leadership how the money was spent; I am not sure. Regular members heard only about the weekly financial crises.

Jane made it clear she was the final say on how the church money was spent. If a member asked to know how the money was spent, they were scoffed. Ask Otto C*. He dared asked about the finances during a service and suffered a scathing rebuke. Later, Jane admitted Otto and his wife loaned the church large sums of money. On one occasion, we were told he loaned the church $50,000. No doubt, he had a personal interest in the finances of the church.

In years past, I was a member of other churches run the same way. Since 1983, I can remember being in three other churches that did not share expenditure reports with members. So, Jane was not alone in her push to keep her financial decisions beyond examination. These three other churches were also of the independent, charismatic Word of Faith beliefs. In contrast, I helped prepare budgets and expenditure reports for a church in Summerville, SC. Why did I not consider disclosure essential at WOFF?

During one evening service, Jane came to the podium. "We need $25,000 to meet the bills in the office. God told me that some folks are saving money for their children. God said to give it."

Within this controlled environment, did this statement cause folks to feel bad or evil if they did not give up their children's inheritance? The leader in supreme authority and who hears God on every matter in your life had declared, "God said to give it."

After the offering was counted, Jane came back to the microphone. She was visibly excited. "We have had a miracle."

The offering was counted and the amount came to $50,000! She shed tears and thanked those folks who had obeyed and heard God say to give the money they were saving for their children. By the offering exceeding the need, it confirmed to Jane she had obeyed God in her "putting it before the people."

One of my first questions was what happened to the extra $25,000? The overage was never mentioned. There was no partial or complete accounting of the offerings taken. Disclosure might lead to more questions. Where was all this money being spent? Once, there was mention that it took $20,000 a week to meet the bills. That figure sounded like a lot of money to me. We never saw a written listing of expenses. If the budget was met every week, where did the approximate one million dollars taken in during a year go? We were told only in general terms about salaries, property insurance and taxes.

One way WOFF cut costs was through security. There were members watching the grounds 24/7. This was supposed to help get a discount on the property and liability insurance. Men or couples volunteered to take shifts overnight. The church liability insurance premium was "high because some folks had made a claim against the church insurance," according to Sam. A couple of incidents were shared in which a member fell and did not have their own insurance. They filed a claim against the church insurance. Names were given. Oh, the imputed shame for using the church insurance. How did that make those members feel?

During one memorable service, Jane freely talked about her own finances. "I receive a check for $600 each month. From that, I give Sam $200."

Sam spoke up, "I squirrel the $200 away for the future."

The impression was the $600 a month equaled Jane's total compensation. The problem with that was vast and obvious. Every member knew of her estate on over forty acres. We remembered her saying that she and Sam had taken out mortgages on every possible property, including their home, to pay attorney bills from a previous legal battle. Jane told us about the shopping trips in North Carolina and Atlanta for dresses and jewelry.

Many of us heard her say at another time, "If all my clothes were laid out, they would cover two city blocks." I am unsure if that included her purses and shoes.

We knew she had a cell phone, television(s) and a large pool. A quick look at her lifestyle bewildered many concerning her ability to make it on $400 a month. Was it reasonable to think the church paid for her house, cars, cell phone, new clothes, trips out of town and other things? Why did we not know for sure? You got it. She expected us to completely trust her because she hears God at such a "high level." Hearing God on how to spend church finances was no big deal.

Jane mentioned more than once that the CPA for the church assured her, "You are more than above board in the use of the ministry money."

Was he also getting paid to perform that service and make those statements? How long would he keep the contract for the church finances if he did not give a glowing report? How much was he *paid*? As members, we were never told. Jane couldn't *afford* to tell us.

While receiving the tithes, Sam made our financial circumstances plain, "If you are not being blessed financially, you are not tithing."

During certain services, people stood up and testified how God was blessing them financially. Many times, this meant buying newer cars and houses.

Sam was a licensed used car dealer. He bought cars at auction for members. According to Sam, he made about $500 a car. In another service, Jane informed us, "If you buy a car from somewhere else, (besides Sam) you are paying too much."

Sam burst with pride as he told about his car buddies circling the church and noting how many "nice cars" (newer) there were in the parking lot. Sam translated this for his friends as "God's blessings on His people."

Douglas McDonald, a leader in the church received a rebuke during a service for not buying his car from Sam.

WOFF leaders lived steeped in the "Prosperity Gospel" message. On one level, I wanted to believe it; on another level, it made no sense. I know now their refusal to disclose the finances of the church to the members kept the mystery of the (financial) gospel alive and available as a tool to harvest more money whenever needed. As long as Jane kept the numbers to herself, she could keep passing the plates always saying we need more to meet "the budget." She ran an efficient cash machine.

CHAPTER THIRTEEN

MEDICAL DEBT COLLECTIONS

In December of 2007 after a Sunday night service, a list of members who needed to report to the fellowship hall was read from the podium. My name was called and, immediately, I tried to figure out the purpose of the meeting based on the other names on the list.

A group of about twenty-five gathered in the room, and Jane Whaley entered. Robin Webster and Suzanna Southerland were already at the front of the room.

Jane started, "(Dr.) Pat Pagter has not taken a salary in two years. I want to talk to those in the church who owe him money."

She was handed a list of names and balances. I did not see the list, but she referenced the printed list. Robin and Suzanna worked for Dr. Pagter, Suzanna's father. Both answered Jane's questions about who was paying and who was not, in front of the whole group. This appeared low key at first, non-threatening on the surface.

Jane addressed individuals calling them by name, telling them how much they owed. Then she asked, "What can you pay?"

Josh Farmer spoke up, "Why am I here?"

"Your grandmother owes a balance."

Immediately, he wrote a check, gave it to Suzanna and huffed as he left the room.

Next, Jane called the name and amount owed for a woman sitting close to the front.

"You owe this amount (she stated it). You have not paid since (she named the date). When can you pay?"

Jane brought the woman's mother, Joan into the conversation, "Why is your daughter not paying?"

The woman recounted her struggles over finding a job.

Jane and Robin chimed in almost at the same time, "It's your fault you can't keep a job; you are a reproach on your job."

Robin went on further. "God has given you several jobs, and you are not grateful. You attack God's plan by the way you act on your job."

Finally, either Jane or Robin told the lady in front of everyone, "If you cannot pay, then find another doctor."

The admonition landed on everyone. Finding another doctor meant going outside the group for medical care. Who wanted to do that? When have *you* ever been loved like this in public?

My name was called, but Suzanna cleared me. "John has been paying every month."

Whew. A few days before, I had sent off a check to pay on the balance. This saved me a royal rebuke...this time. Each person's information was reviewed by Jane. She did not call out the names of some people who were present for whatever reason.

What is wrong with this meeting? My work background for most of thirty plus years has been in consumer debt collection. My training includes listening to several attorneys speak on the **Fair Debt Collection Practices Act** (FDCPA), as well as the **Health Insurance Portability and Accountability Act (HIPAA) of 1996**. Though I have never been cited for violations of these two acts, I have seen others who were accused of such violations.

In my opinion, this meeting was a blatant violation of both FDCPA and HIPAA. Jane, Robin and Suzanna violated the rights of everyone in the room. They excused this meeting as an effort to "help a friend."

The privacy of each person was violated. In my opinion, the audacity of Jane Whaley to call out individuals, revealing their medical debts in front of others was stunning. Mr. Farmer's reaction made it clear; she did not seek any counsel from him as to the legality of the meeting. He might have redirected her efforts.

If anyone had questioned Jane about this meeting, they risked being shunned or put out. I left the meeting in total shock. Power plays from Jane were common. We witnessed them many times in different situations. This meeting was the most blatant and shameless announcement of absolute power and disregard for a member's personal and financial privacy that I witnessed in my sixteen years of involvement. Of course, it was all wrapped up in good intentions.

CHAPTER FOURTEEN

FUND RAISERS, FUND RAISERS AND MORE FUND RAISERS

L ife in this group always included fund raising projects of one kind or another. My wife was the coordinator for fund raisers for the school and, in some cases, for the church. This gave me a close up view of many of the fund raising projects including the process of product selection. The frequent fund-raising was not new to us. In Greenville, we were well aware of the fund raising needs. Once we moved to Spindale, it became more of an emphasis than ever before.

During the decision process, my wife received information in the mail and reviewed the proposed fundraiser for certain criteria. The criteria was not written, you had to "hear by the Spirit" if this product or idea worked.

How did some projects get eliminated? We did not sell anything that was on the "don't list." After we stopped celebrating holidays, a lot of projects went straight into the trash can. No more greeting cards, no more gift wrap, no holiday candles, no holiday candy. For some reason, we could sell poinsettias, though it was considered a holiday flower. There was at least one time where we sold Easter lilies.

A fund raising project started with Friday night fellowship dinners. As a comparison, in Greenville, we had fund raisers during Tuesday night fellowship dinners. In these dinners we learned the spiritual privilege to *pay* for the food we brought. In Spindale on Friday nights, we were allowed to repeat that fun and bring food and then pay to eat it. I agree that makes no sense.

Eventually, we were told in both places, if you did not have the money then don't worry, still come and eat. The catch? You walked past the lady taking the money. How embarrassing it was to walk by and say you can't pay today. Sometimes, I wanted to ask if I could take some money *out* of the bag, but that was foolishness, a big no-no.

If you arrived at the fellowship dinners after the initial flood of members, you may receive little to eat. Often I arrived late, stopping to eat on the way there. This took several times of showing up at the church and leaving hungry for me to learn this approach. That left me with the options of buying something to eat elsewhere or warming up leftovers at home. I had another reason for not eating at the church; members brought food that was cheap and quick to fix, including large amounts of fast food: fried, fat-filled and greasy.

The church ran a snack bar in the fellowship building for many years. In addition to drinks, candy, cookies and chips, it also carried make-up. For years, the snack bar sold books, Bibles and notebooks, too. Early on, the church sold cassette tapes of the services.

There were other items for sale from time to time. One member, Leigh Valentine, had a representative in the snack bar ready to sell her make-up. The make-up sale sounded so spiritual, yet it seemed out of place.

An epic fund raising attempt involved Leigh Valentine's "Living the Life" products. Leigh had a product line for which the church could supply the marketing and telephone support. The plan included member-staffed phone banks for a special promotion. Leigh had a contract with QVC® which paid her much more than the average church member's salary. She "heard God" to offer this project as a fundraiser in order to help the church.

Jane told us, "There is no guarantee, but Leigh has a big following on QVC. The church could maybe make a million dollars with this make up."

Wow! That statement had lots of members giving in to loose talk, eyes bugging out, the ladies drooling and the men standing around saying, "What did she just say?"

The preparation for this fund raiser took several weeks, requiring many hours of free labor setting up the phone banks. I was not involved with the physical preparations, but I did participate in the training along with other members. Women needed training to answer the phones and take make-up orders. During the set-up and training, the husbands of the order takers called in and pretended to order make-up. These calls were the closest thing we experienced to playing on the telephone.

The phones were staffed 24/7 for several weeks. The numbers of order takers varied according to when the infomercials aired. Like a balloon losing air, this fund raiser never got off the ground. Each night, eager ladies sat in their cubicles waiting by the phones, but few calls came. They fell way short of earning a million dollars. I don't remember the exact sales numbers, someone had missed God. This one was a true bust. I feel sure someone blamed it on a devil of some type. This fiasco may have contributed to Leigh Valentine filing bankruptcy in 2006.

Our yard sale and consignment sale fund raisers were more successful and consistent. Those responsible for them learned the governing regulations and moved the sales around to different properties in order to stay within the rules. On Wednesday night after the service, we set up tents and brought in large items from all over the county. The items we donated were no longer needed or were determined as no longer God's will. Some of the businesses in the church donated items. People donated furniture, clothes, contraband items, old toys and more. Pricing was dirt cheap. This brought in the traffic. Customers did not know they were buying God's leftovers.

We were told to be careful over what we bought at the yard sale. It was in the yard sale for a reason. You had to "hear God" if it was yours. You might end up with it for no charge or a minimal price.

We were warned, "Do not buy ties at the yard sale." Brooke made sure those who did were embarrassed over a tie that was "no longer God's will." Apparently, God's taste in ties changed with the seasons or some other indicator.

Yard sales lasted until Saturday afternoon. We needed lots of helpers to set things up and take things down. Afterward, members in charge decided to store certain items for the next sale or send them off to a local shelter ministry. The unwanted items were hauled to the dump.

Sometimes, we held flower sales. Ray Farmer traveled to wholesalers with a long trailer to purchase flowers. These sales occurred before Mother's Day or Easter or some other occasion. Yes, we did not celebrate those holidays but did not mind taking people's money if they chose to celebrate pagan days.

At some point, snack sales started before or after evening services. These included non-healthy, quick, snack foods. We did so much at the church; why not eat more meals there, too? Members donated baked goods and then turned around and bought them back for a fund raiser. These bake sales were, of course, after you left a service where they may have passed the plate three or four times to meet the church budget.

While a member, I did not dwell on how many opportunities there were to harvest money from regular members. There was no benefit in keeping count.

As many other churches do, we held car wash fundraisers at the church property. Members signed up for a time slot to come get their car washed. The cost was $15 for a wash and thorough vacuum. The catch? If your car was too dirty or had contraband, you were asked about it. Did you not wash it more than once a year? Of course, if you did not keep your appointment, you may get a call. There was still a slot open for you. If the proceeds were for the school and you were a parent of school-aged children, you were expected to help with the labor.

There were other fund raisers which included fruit sales. This event always caused a big issue on how to properly coordinate the delivery to customers before the fruit rotted. The person in charge ordered extra, so someone had to sell it to others or to other church members.

For a few years, doughnut sales were common in the colder months. Someone made early morning trips to the bakery an hour away, and then we got out of bed early on Saturday to start hawking the round fat wheels. You knew at some point people came to their senses and decided they did not want round fat wheels. Alas, left over boxes were sold the next day after the church service. Have no fear; someone will take them home. It was for a good cause: the school or the church. They were showing their support for God's will.

WOFF had a designated church photographer. He worked a construction job and took the pictures for church members as a side business. He had a guaranteed clientele and did a good job. He took engagement pictures, wedding pictures, and pictures for graduations, memorial services or any other special service or gathering. He, also, took family pictures. I suppose that got dicey when so many families split up. Every year, he took the school pictures. These were sold as a fund raiser for the school. Be aware, you did not buy the copyrights, only the hard copies. Don't scan them and send them to relatives. You were corrected for that.

Other fund raisers included practical items such as first aid kits. At times, certain members purchased new clothes in large lots and sold them for a mark-up as a fund raiser. For a long while, there was an ongoing consignment clothes sale at the church. We sold higher end clothes that had not been deemed out of the will of God. Also, there were occasional purse sales. The purse you purchased had to match the gift of God in you and then you needed shoes.

For the men, clothing fundraisers included the sales of suits and ties. Someone in clothes leadership either bought a large number of suits or took pre-orders for suits. Members were encouraged to dress according to the gift of God in you. Why not use this requirement to make money? It made total WOFF sense.

There were larger fundraiser projects. These included one member buying a foreclosed home in another state and getting church labor to repair and make it ready to sell. The church might make $30,000 or more on a house.

Again, there was no financial disclosure, I never saw a printout of what these fund raisers netted or how the money was devoured. I wondered if there was a black hole in Jane's office that could only be appeased with bundles of cash. As soon as money was raised, this black hole sucked it right out the door into the never-never-land to pay for or buy something only Jane-knew-what.

Oh, we are not done my friend.

Fund raising projects included working for others in the community who needed painting or work around their home. I don't know if we received money every time, but, at times, we were told the church received donations for the services provided.

This has been a brief recap of the many fundraising efforts of WOFF. When considering this money machine, we must remember the countless hours of free labor provided by church members. Yes, I know it is accepted practice for folks to donate their time to non-profit organizations. In many other non-profit groups, they provide some sort of financial accounting to explain how the money comes in and how it goes out. Our members were conditioned to not expect this common courtesy. They were expected to trust Jane heard from God on everything. Why should the decisions on spending money be any different? It was all part of the required complete trust package.

Other Financial Issues

A few months ago, I heard a well-known financial expert on the radio discussing family finances. He finished the discussion about the family budget making the statement that it was okay to tell your children you could not afford something they wanted.

The phrase "we cannot afford that right now" caught my attention. Why? While inside WOFF, we were taught to not say that phrase to our children. It "hurts their faith." This edict put parents in a precarious position and resulted in strained family budgets. If an item was *approved* and others were buying it, whatever it was, then there was great pressure to come up with the funds and buy it. We were told to go to church leadership and ask for help to get it.

What did this do for the children? In my opinion, it gave them an unrealistic idea of financial provision for family finances. This led to thinking, "If my parents can't buy it, maybe someone else in the church will." We were talking about wants, not needs. I did not see anyone go lacking for real needs, but, the dress shoes, the church clothes, the toys or other wants—that was a different matter. The "prosperity message" was taught early to the children. "Extend your faith, believe God, and keep believing..."

We were told: "After all, God is not limited to your paycheck."

God may not be, but, when bills are due, extras might need to wait. Jane could always send the offering plates around "one more time, until we get it." What we taught our children was not a true picture of how things work in a family budget. When the paycheck came up short, I did not go back to my employer and "pass the plate." By not saying "we cannot afford that right now," we exposed our children to the same religious mess that many of the adults lived in.

This surreal, false, religious practice did not help the children know the difference between needs and wants. Combine this with the added unspoken guilt on parents for not celebrating birthdays and Christmas, and you have a picture of the many dilemmas of living in a closed religious group. You learned Jane's way or the highway.

Why should members expect reality in the way Jane handled finances? She reported to no one and made all the money decisions herself. Why should members expect prudent, responsible, open financial accounting?

CHAPTER FIFTEEN

LANDMARK CHURCH SERVICES

The following services marked a proverbial bend in the road. We did not know where the road was leading, but down this road we were led. As part of life inside, we expected to experience "new places" in God. New events, new dynamics and new revelations lost their uniqueness. Every service might hold something new; therefore, new became normal. We were living "in the move of God."

These narratives are not grouped in any particular time order or importance. I've selected ones I find vital to explaining the dynamics of the subculture of WOFF. I lived these narratives.

We will start with one of my all-time favorites: The Toilet Paper Revelation.

From the podium, out of nowhere, Jane said, "God told me the right way to put the toilet paper on the roll."

She continued on to other matters then came back to this. "Do you want to know what God said?"

Members nodded. No doubt her impression was we all wanted to know.

Jane explained that while she was in the bathroom, she heard God tell her the right way to put the toilet paper on the roll. She confidently declared the right way was the paper rolling "over the top."

"Do you want to know why? There is less wasted, than if the paper rolls from underneath."

She added that God had been dealing with her about folding the end of the paper when she was finished, like they do in hotels. I do not recall the exact date of this revelation; however, who could forget such an essential, life-enhancing revelation from the Apostle Jane Whaley? This essential gold nugget was not only talked about that day, it became the buzz in the church for several days.

The fallout from this service was no less than amazing. True to form, children scrutinized the paper habits of others in their household. There were self-appointed "TP Police." Some were more vocal than others. Can you imagine the thoughts when you were finished? Now, do I fold or do I not fold? The choice even more vital to life: when it's your turn to change the roll, do you go over or under? Do you believe the newest revelation is from the "Throne" or not?

The foray around making sure everyone completed the requirements for toilet paper roll direction and folding neatness became comical. The pressure to be on the right side of this revelation intensified. Members lived in multi-family households. This made your bathroom habits visible by more than your immediate family. The toilet paper pressure became greater and greater. People even worried over the question of bringing the paper to a symmetrical fold with a neat point and how to best accomplish that. Lessons were available.

Jane Whaley came to the podium a couple of weeks later to moderate the frenzy. She pointed out that conversations had gotten out of hand. She reminded folks that she had shared what God told her. It did not mean God required the same thing for each one of us. Whew! Maybe the bathroom inspections would be less intense. Gradually, the frenzy died away. But to this day, I still hear that question, over or under? I have stopped feeling the pressure to fold.

Why bring this up? The more accurate question is: Why did Jane bring this up? What could be the basis for Jane feeling justified in expressing her revelation in this area? Over and over, I heard the following scripture given when addressing small details of daily life inside:

[5]Behold! God is mighty, and yet despises no one nor regards anything as trivial...

(Job 36:5 AMP)

The whole line of conversation seemed odd. This serves as evidence of Jane's compulsions to control members' everyday life. The effects these revelations from God had on members were amazing. If the controls stopped with mere toilet paper etiquette, we would have little reason to continue. However, we keep going.

Along this same area of wisdom, from the podium, Gerald Southerland commented that his shampoo bottle included a "new age" statement.

He proclaimed, "I did not pay it any attention."

Suddenly, Jane spoke up, "Get rid of it. You don't need a new age shampoo."

Gerald had a military background and knew how to do an about face.

He quickly explained, "I am ready to get a new shampoo."

Some of the members chuckled, but it was plain that Gerald had yet again met the "authority of God." Members met the authority of God in various ways. That day it happened to be over shampoo.

What were the results of this edict? You already know. This gave folks yet something else to check for in your bathroom, added to toilet paper direction, wiping the sink before you left the bathroom and other rules during your personal time. Checking behind each other was a major task and essential responsibility for members. Does this sound like an inviting place to live?

Vividly, I remember one Sunday morning service in Greenville right after a seminar in Spindale. We re-preached the seminar message to those in Greenville who had not attended.

That evening, Jane asked, "Gerald, tell us about your morning service in Greenville?"

"We shared what God did in the seminar."

"You missed God!"

How did she know? That morning, they had a move of God doing something different. The immediate understanding, if God moved for WOFF, we missed God by doing anything else. I remember feeling so embarrassed by being in the group who missed God. We did not even know anything until Jane revealed the very breath of God to us. Oh, where can I hide? Jane's wisdom came to us frequently in many different ways.

A Sunday evening prior to 2002, Jane Whaley held up a set of camping toys. These were left on the previous Friday night in one of the classrooms. She wanted to "help the people" learn Jesus.

"Who did this?"

She did not wait for someone to admit the sin.

She exclaimed, "We don't allow these toys. It teaches our children that playing with fire is okay."

Finally, the pressure overwhelmed my wife. Martha stood up, interrupting Jane to admit our gross sin. "Jane, those are our son's toys."

Jane in her loving, caring attitude snapped back, "I knew who did it! I was not going to say it in front of everyone."

Jane used this scene to further establish her power as sole authority on children and their toys. My wife sat back down and finished taking her scolding in the privacy of her own thoughts. I sat in my chair replaying the events in my mind. We were experiencing a preview of God's ways among His chosen people. We were being "loved on" the WOFF way.

Similar scenes evolved with play tools.

"We don't let our children have those. They will confuse them with real tools and could get cut or hurt handling a real tool when no one is looking."

When was that possible? Children were never left alone at any point during those years.

"Don't leave them alone, the devil is waiting to attack them."

May Seminar- We Watched Other Ministers...

One service for a May seminar, we walked into the sanctuary to find there were television monitors set up. This was a rare event: allowing us to watch anything on monitors (televisions). I only remember a few times when monitors were used. We watched scenes from the 911 attack and Ronald Reagan's funeral. We watched Tammy Faye Bakker's last interview with Larry King. We were shown the History Channel's "History of Christmas" tape. We watched speeches by President George W. Bush, weddings in Brazil and Africa, and a few other events. As a rule, regular members did not have televisions in their homes. Some in leadership may have had televisions. Jane had a television God told her to watch.

The congregation buzzed with excitement. The buzz quieted as Jane came to the podium. The anxious expectations were tangible.

She announced, "God wanted to show us just what else is out there in the Body of Christ. I have taped some ministry shows off Christian television for us to watch. You need to guard yourself so some of the messages don't come into you. There are places where the music has been muted. It was so bad, so profane."

With those warnings, the monitors were turned on. Jane sat on the front row with the remote in her hand.

I do not remember every minister on the tape; however, I do remember my impressions during the viewing. Jane taped several preachers, many African American. The sad part was hearing the snickers and muffled laughter in the congregation. Jane narrated with a microphone. She admitted if she knew the speaker or other reasons why she chose to record them.

Members from several other churches were in this meeting. I did not look around to see who was amused and showing their glee. The fact that the laughing continued unrestrained, fed the attitude, "we are special; we don't carry on in that way."

This video montage confirmed the belief: "We know there are others with Truth; we just have not found them yet." We must be of God since we don't do those things, right?

At times like these, it was hard for me to believe we were the only ones with "Truth." The snickering and laughter was sad. How many years previous to this had the entire country been privy to the scenes of WOFF prayer groups filmed by *Inside Edition*? Many outsiders watching those videos believed, "we don't carry on like that."

The church from Michigan broke ties with WOFF as a result of this seminar. Though I knew a few in that church, I was not in the meetings that preceded their departure. Most of them were African American. Possibly, they took exception with the content and prevailing attitude during that meeting. After this seminar, a few African American members came to the podium telling of their former participation in services similar to the ones we watched. All of this fed on itself and furthered the elitist attitude.

This break with the Michigan church contributed to another event. One morning, I went to the church office to drop off some papers. When I arrived, I found each office worker crying, sniffling and turning away to hide tears. *Who died?*

I did not ask about the tears. Later, I found out a father from Michigan came to town that morning to retrieve his son from the church and school. Law enforcement officials were with him to carry out his request. The young man was seventeen years old. There was a judge's order to release the school records.

This father had done his homework. The young man was taken back to Michigan. Later, he spent time at Wellspring Retreat in Ohio. After he turned eighteen, he came back claiming he was put out of Wellspring because he refused treatment. This was a badge of honor for him. He has since married a church member, remaining in the church.

Dr. Z

During my sixteen years of WOFF influence, I remember one visiting minister speaking from the pulpit. This did not include the numerous politicians from the local or state levels coming to court the vote. This number did not include the ministers from other churches within the fellowship.

The one visiting minster was Dr. Z from Africa. We were told we could not pronounce his real name, so he was addressed as Dr. Z. Jane met him on an airplane trip and invited him to visit. Who knows what her true motives were? However, after he had spoken and left the building, she gave us a laundry list of his flaws. We could not count his message to be on the same level as hers. He did not receive with gladness the prayer offered him before he left and besides, "He was not walking where we are walking."

The underlying message was that Jane walked *in a higher place in the spirit* and to think otherwise was foolish. She was superior in "the things of God."

We heard many messages on the subject of repentance; however, the only times I heard Jane repent was for mispronouncing a name or a word. Jane did not lead by example, unless, of course, she never sinned. This was confusing. She had fits and screamed at members during services. We were told to leave her alone; God must be angry with us since Jane was His messenger.

Many times, I heard her come into a service screaming, "The sin in here makes me sick!"

After that declaration, the joy was hard to show on our faces and many cowered in fear. The thoughts bore down on us: "What did I do?" "Is it my turn to be blasted?"

We also knew, for your sake; please don't get up to use the bathroom during a service: "You should have done that before the service."

Going to the bathroom before services was always a big deal; lines were long.

Falling asleep or nodding during a service was also sinful.

Jane declared: "That sleep devil is attacking some in here. Stand up and move to the back so you can hear the Word. You may miss the very word that could keep you from going to hell."

"Your sin affects me!"

The first Sunday service during a November seminar, Jane learned of a senior citizen going to the local grocery stores and picking up advertising fliers for other members.

Jane looked befuddled, "No one told me about that."

She ordered the lady to stand up. This lady was more than half way back in the sanctuary and not far from me. Jane yelled a few more words. This member stood shaking, overwhelmed with fear.

Jane turned to leave the room but not before she screamed so all could feel it, "Your sin affects me! What you do in this community is a reflection of me!"

The member's best intention mattered not. The lady collapsed in a heap crying. She went into discipleship, segregated from others until she found a place of repentance. This drama provides another example of the pervasive fear-based control used by Jane.

You are all homely!

During a Sunday evening service in May of 2008, we held a practice for the high school graduation. All of the seniors stood across the front edge of the stage. The graduating class included twelve young ladies. Jane cleared her throat and turned to confer with her daughter.

Then Jane declared, "Every young lady up there is homely."

Snickers flowed through the congregation.

"You all need help."

Her daughter chimed in, "They all look like they are from the Church of God."

Consider the scenario: high school girls getting ready to graduate being told by the principal of their school, the Apostle of the church, the supreme leader having all of the power for everything, and her daughter agreeing, they were all homely. Was this the love of God that Jane had preached for years? Here is the definition of homely: Not attractive or good-looking: a homely child. There was much more than looks at stake here.

After the meeting, to no one's surprise, appearances changed for the senior girls. Up until that meeting, girls under eighteen years old did not have pierced ears or use colored nail polish. Also, eye-liner was reserved for those over eighteen. Under the age of eighteen, girls were allowed to use foundation, light blush, lipstick of certain colors, and clear nail polish, but no eye color. In the next few days, teased-up hair, French tips and pierced ears became the order of business. Things changed in order to chase away the "homely" and "COG" look. The excitement generated to please Jane bordered on bizarre. What was the standard shown to these young ladies? What was the goal?

During the second part of that service, one of the other school principals, Jenna Cason*, berated the parents for allowing these girls to leave the house in such a homely condition.

She exclaimed, "You don't love your daughter if you let her walk around homely."

Most of the twelve girls' parents sat in the second meeting. I did not have warm, fuzzy, love of God feelings that night. Weren't we following the rules that Jane had heard from God up until that point? Who or what had changed?

The graduation pictures showed the results. Yes, homely was run out the door. But, at what cost? Jane's priorities were crystal clear at this meeting. Did homely girls hurt her reputation?

No one nailed it to the core, except Jane.

Before we moved from Greenville, during a service about fifty members at a time were gathered from the sanctuary into the fellowship hall. We were directed to come in and be seated. Anxious thoughts: *What had we all done? What was the common sin in every-one?*

We did not have to wait long. This was no ordinary take hold, shouting, rebuking, and puking session.

We were seated, the doors closed. A letter was read aloud. It was written by one of the high school graduates for their college admissions application.

Jane asked "If you think this letter was written by the Spirit of God, then stand up."

Leaders at the front of the room demanded, "Decide quickly!"

Some folks stood. Jane asked a few of the ones standing and a few of those who remained seated to tell why they gave their answer. After a couple of people explained their thoughts, Jane told us how the letter came to her attention. She immediately knew the letter was not of God. She decided to read it to her leadership as a test and, now, to regular members.

She continued, "I want to know who can hear God and see the worldly attitudes reflected in the letter."

Jane continued, expressing disappointment with the person who wrote the letter, a graduate of the WOFF Christian School.

Jane declared, "I was shocked that this young person still had the love of the world. She is now under the strong dealings of God. She may not even attend college with that in her heart. College would take her over!"

That day, in my group of fifty, we were all wrong. Even those who had answered correctly did not explain why the letter wasn't of God in exact terms to satisfy her requirement.

Jane declared, "You all still have the love of education and the world's ways. Not one of you has been able to nail to the core the deception and wickedness in this letter!"

Had Jane Whaley accomplished her purpose?

She was the *only one* who could see the level of evil. Jane lived as the final authority on sin. This test was yet another way to keep her top position. It furthered the insecure feelings and groveling behavior in some members.

How could anyone make it without Jane? Her always crystal clear discernment of God and His ways saves us.

Later, the deceived young lady stood before the church to repent. She thanked Jane for "hitting her sin" and repeated other WOFF mantras of Jane worship.

This method of public humiliation was common, producing the results Jane desired. Members could not hide in a group; they were often singled out and rebuked in the service. Jane and other members of leadership were given authority to correct others.

The young lady who wrote the letter now serves as one of the church lawyers. Since Jane allowed this person to attend college and law school, she must have her breakthrough. If she had never written such an evil letter, the deception might still be on us all.

Stop taking notes...

Note taking was not allowed during services. In earlier years, we wrote all the notes we wanted. WOFF notebooks were sold in the snack bar. The practice changed when a church secretary came to the podium. She called the name of a young man, saying she read his notebook. We knew she was helping this young fellow and his family. The woman spoke to Jane as she told her observations for us all to hear.

"Jane, as I looked around during the preaching, folks were taking notes and not paying attention to the WORD. Taking notes is a distraction."

In order to prove her point, she read aloud from the young man's notebook. Yes, these were his personal notes. They were for his consumption and reflection, not others. The content of the pages was not the issue here.

With this discovery of inattentiveness, Jane instantly banned note taking during services. The only approved note taking was of scripture references—no dates, no names, no personal reflections—nothing but scripture references. We were not allowed to add anything to the references.

How did this affect the members? As with the toilet paper revelation, the immediate effect was predictable. Many of the ones who were the "TP Police" were now the "Note Nazis." They sprang up everywhere. We were encouraged to watch our neighbor, make sure they were "taking hold" of the new dictates. Being watched for such details was a consuming feeling, a part of WOFF-life in so many areas.

Several children took special interest in their ability to critique and report adult behavior. In one service, a young boy told his mom that a visiting Brazilian was taking notes during the singing. The mom felt the usual pressure to keep the rules, making sure she reported any transgressions.

The mom stood up, getting Jane's attention, "Jane, (she called the Brazilian's name) is taking notes."

Jane called him forward to talk to him. He appeared flustered as he walked forward to explain himself.

After a short conference, Jane explained, "It is okay, he is taking notes for the songs to take them back to his church in Brazil."

Tensions diffused.

However, the commandment to keep watching the behavior of everyone in the service became crystal clear. No one was exempt from scrutiny.

The ban on note taking went along with increased control over the audio or video tapes of the services. Since the media and legal attack in 1995, the process for getting tapes of services was tightly controlled. First, you had to sign the tapes out. You could take them with you but warned not to leave them in your car. "That could open the church up to an attack."

Soon the rules stated you could not take the tapes off of the property. You listened to them on church grounds. People missing a service or many of the folks on church discipline were required to listen to the service they missed. During a weeklong seminar, tapes of the morning services or previous services were played after the evening service. If you missed a service, you were expected to stay after the evening service and watch or listen to the tape.

Don't read it...

In July of 2006, Jayne Caulder, the church secretary, came into the sanctuary and shared an article in the local paper about Leigh Valentine filing bankruptcy. She had appeared in the local bankruptcy court. Jayne, Leigh, her company secretary and another man attended the court session. A synopsis of the article which originally appeared in the Daily Courier, USA on July 23, 2006 is found here: (http://www.religionnewsblog.com/15355/bankruptcy-filing-reveals-ties-to-word-of-faith-fellowship)

The church secretary explained in brief the content of the article, and then she told us, "Don't read it. It's about Leigh's bankruptcy and there is a bunch of stuff in there that is not true."

She waved her hand toward the congregation as if to say don't waste your time. It was nothing to be concerned about. Since no quotes from the article were provided, it caught my interest. Within a couple of days, I found a copy online.

My occupation required me to learn about bankruptcy. I knew the basic proceedings and the filing of schedules. I was not a lawyer and did not know all of the details of Leigh Valentine's case, but she was a part of WOFF for several years. The circumstances surrounding her involvement raised questions for me. As mentioned in a previous chapter, her make-up was sold on church property.

Something in the article did strike me as odd. During the hearing, Ms. Valentine was asked about a claim submitted in the case. The Judge asked her about a claim for $32,500 submitted by David and Jayne Caulder. Leigh replied, at first, she was not sure about the debt, and then she suggested that it was for child care expenses. She traveled back and forth to Texas. The Caulders kept her son. She declared under oath, she owed this debt to Jayne and David Caulder for child-care.

The claim the Caulders filed against Leigh for thousands of dollars she owed for childcare shocked me. The odd fact was during my time inside, no one that I knew charged for childcare. We kept each other's children. Likewise, when needed, others returned the favor. I never remember money changing hands for childcare. No one ever ap-proached me for money to keep my children. When a child stayed with another family during meal time, we discussed beforehand how the expense of the meal was to be handled. You might give money for their meal, but it was not intended for the time spent taking care of your children. Children spent the night with our family and vice versa with no mention of money changing hands. This give and take oc-curred, at least in the group of regular members which I knew.

The Caulders were one of the wealthiest families in the church. David Caulder worked as a well-respected, well known realtor. Why did they charge Leigh Valentine thousands of dollars for childcare? And allow Leigh to list a claim for it on her bankruptcy schedules? On top of that, they let her swear to the court that all the information in the schedules was true and accurate. These two wealthy families may have had an arrangement that was different from how regular mem-bers of lesser financial status treated each other. For sure, there could be no intention of inflating Leigh's debts in order to skew her finan-cial situation. Right, no way. All parties were true and honest and above board. The Bonars also kept Leigh's son when she traveled. Hopefully, they were able to get in on that deal. I sure hope so, though they never mentioned it.

This occurrence has been a mystery to me for years. While in the group, my first reflex was to believe everyone, including leadership, always told the truth. How else could you stay a member, unless you had confidence in words being spoken from the podium? I suspect other members believed Jayne about the article. After I read the article, my blind faith in leadership or Jane Whaley was replaced with a new vision. An uneasy shadow of doubt began to grow in me after this episode.

The Love of God

Jane stated "Everyone loves Jane Whaley and Jane loves everyone. If they don't (love Jane) then they are listening to devils."

She uttered more about the Love of God, "The love of God is the love of God." Jane went on to explain, "I love Sam and Opie** the same. It is the same love. I just show that love differently to Sam."

At another time, she talked about folks who had left and how she loved them all. "Well, there may be two folks if I saw them walking down the street, I would cross over so I didn't have to speak to them. Only two or maybe three."

Again, these statements may not be in time order, but the meaning is clear. The first statement is revealing all by itself. For Jane to say that *if you don't love her, you are listening to devils,* reflected her overwhelming modesty and humility, right? All indications suggested Jane believed this about herself. She believed these truisms should positively affect others.

Concerning the second statement, I remember the service when she uttered those words. She said this could be misunderstood, and she quickly added the part about showing the love of God differently to Sam. No further explanation was given, and the impression for me was not much "different."

The third statement ignited curiosity over who had made Jane angry enough that she refused to meet them on the street. In public, Jane can be the sweetest thing since jelly toast, but for her to admit she was so upset with someone seemed strange. Well, not so strange since she referenced those who left as those who "betrayed God." This left the list of possibilities wide open.

As in other matters, we were not allowed to talk about these statements between each other unless our conversations were to encourage others to act in accordance with the nugget of truth. No one dared express any doubt or the slightest hint of disbelief or critical attitude about Jane, her life, her words or her decisions. She lived as god.

Don't go talking about this service...

Sunday evening meetings often included the discussion of church family matters. Issues were addressed in an open forum. Jane asked a question or introduced a scenario, and then she opened the podium for others to ask questions or tell what they saw during a situation. Families and households might be called up front to stand while the situation was discussed. These meetings included public rebukes for anyone in attendance or listening to the service over the phone. Other important events were announced during the Sunday evening meetings such as engagements or pending births.

One Sunday service, Jane said, "I think we have an announcement."

A couple came to the podium and reactions of glee rippled through the congregation. Many folks expressed happiness at the pending announcement. This couple was older than the normal age range for first marriages. The fellow became a member a few years earlier. He had experienced several serious emotional events and had lived through many struggles and changes. The woman came from Texas where she worked on the staff of a large church. Now, she worked on our church staff. He worked selling granite at a church-member-owned company. They were friends for a while before this announcement. As he went through struggles, she supported him in approved ways. Their relationship included a few ministry trips together with other members. This engagement announcement was not a surprise.

Next, another older couple walked to the podium announcing, "God has shown us we are to be married." The man was quite animated, asking Jane if they could get married soon.

Jane replied, "You still have to walk out a relationship and get some more breakthroughs."

Filled with glee at the thought of one day being married, just not as soon as he wanted, he made a comical gesture of disappointment.

The flurry of the next few announcements caught many by surprise. While we sang and offered prayers of thankfulness, members started going to Jane and speaking in her ear, a common practice. Some kneeled before her. Men and women of all ages made their way to the front. Jane soon allowed the news to be told. These couples told Jane that God had shown them who their mate was to be. When Jane "had a release" about it, she nodded a signal for the couple to walk to the podium. Each couple expressed what they had heard about their relationship with the underlying understanding this relationship may lead to marriage.

The couples kept coming and coming one after another. The flood gates opened as the waves of excitement washed over the congregation. Some were in shock, most showed gleeful approval. The congregations' reactions increased into a crescendo until everyone clapped and thanked God. By the end of the service, there were twenty-one couples engaged. Most of them were first acknowledged by Jane in this meeting. Each one checked it out with Jane before moving to the podium to share the news. Some were friends for a while, some couples had never spent time together; they had obeyed God.

Before the service ended, Jane exhorted us, "This is not a service to go out in the community and talk about. Some folks will not understand God's ways."

What caused the concern? Some couples were under the legal age of consent. Some voiced a desire to marry a person they had never spent any time with. Jane explained she was not sure about some of the younger couples of high school age, especially the ones in eleventh grade.

Jane continued, "I will carry the whole situation and see where God will take it. Don't go talking loosely about what God has done here."

This service was hard for me to understand. The behaviors displayed seemed strange even though I was in the group for years. WOFF had been correctly accused of closely regulating the personal, intimate lives of married couples. So, how was this news of impromptu relationships understood within the surrounding community? Several of these folks have been married since this service. I have no updates on the young high-school-age folks who declared, "God told us to be married."

Before the service closed, Jane announced that one man was already on the phone calling his son who had left the church. He told him if he was still in the church, God may have given him a mate. This entire scene was one of the strangest services I ever experienced. This was the only service I remember Jane stating she wanted kept secret.

CHAPTER SIXTEEN

WOFF REDEFINED RITUALS NO HOLIDAYS

The prohibitions over celebrating holidays evolved over time. The church does not officially admit to celebrating any holidays. Recently, I was told there is more freedom allowed for family time on Thanksgiving. I feel sure the prohibition on eating turkey on that day is still in place. That rule made for creative meals on Thanksgiving. We had spaghetti for one Thanksgiving meal.

The first holiday to be jettisoned was Halloween. Celebrating demonic things did not fit with the direction God had for us or any other churches that followed the lead of Jane Whaley. "It is not wise to make light of demons." How could you celebrate the main thing you were casting out of your members? The odd part? Jane admitted to being a fan of Halloween candy. She advocated it was okay to buy it on clearance the day after Halloween and eat to your heart's content. Candy corn!

Next, Valentine's Day got the axe. "Why if you knew the roots of the tradition (Greek mythology), you would not allow it in your home."

The pattern was set. Research soon commenced on the origins of other holidays.

The church's website explains the stance on holidays:

We do not believe in nor practice the celebration of pagan holidays such as Halloween, Christmas, Easter, Valentine's Day, birthdays, etc. After researching the history of each of these, we found that these all originated from the worship of demons and other gods, truly pagan worship. Their origin came from demon and devil worship, not from God.

(found here- http://www.wordoffaithfellowship.org/our-church/beliefs viewed 06/01/2015)

The stance remains an odd characteristic of the group. I realize in this country, we have the right to participate or not participate in holidays. We are not required and should not be required to participate in any national, regional or cultural celebration regardless of its origin. Freedom to opt out or *in* is still a freedom. It is a freedom in the society at large. Individual choice is the governing factor, freedom to make the choice unhindered by religious pressures from a leader who controls every aspect of her member's lives down to bathroom habits. How much freedom of choice exists in this group? Not much.

Mother's Day

I do not faithfully celebrate every holiday. This is my choice. My focus has transitioned from the details of each holiday to spending time with ones I love and enjoying time together. The fast-paced life of the American culture leaves little time for spending days with those we love and who are important to us. Please, understand Mother's Day made it to the demon worship list. For years, I obeyed the non-celebration requirement. Difficult as that sounds, this was the price paid for membership in the group. I see the price as unreal and too high. For years, I experienced "holiday guilt."

The *effect* of not celebrating Mother's Day for those whose mother was not in the group resulted in severe strain and, in some cases, severance of the relationship. For many years, I never sent my mother, grandmother, or mother-in-law a card or gift. That included Mother's Day or birthdays or Valentine's Day. It was not considered right to buy a card and flowers for your wife, the *mother* of your children. The reason? You may give over to perversion. Translated: you may not consider your first allegiance to the "will of God" at WOFF. In my opinion, severing family ties with those outside the group was essential to solidifying the control over members. Not celebrating holidays was one avenue to accomplish this objective.

The cutting of ties with family or friends centered on the group-related **revelation and practices** which the family outside did not choose to observe or believe. One person related the experience of their sibling cutting off family contact because of a television playing in their parent's home. It was said this church member did not return to visit his parents for years, because the parents left the television playing during the last visit. I knew the struggle. Church members were coached by Jane or leadership on situations with outside family members. At times, this coaching occurred in front of the whole church. This set an example of "walking in the revelation God has given" and "to sanctify God before the people."

Is there surprise WOFF does not recognize the celebration of Fathers' Day? Remember the matriarchal structure? If mothers were left out on their day, then fathers had no chance. In order to continue at WOFF, you gave up your choice to *opt in* on several issues related to family life.

The Fourth of July

Taking the stand with WOFF about holidays became a rite of passage and members wore it as a badge of honor. The choice made to not "eat at the demon's table" translated into an outward sign of an inward allegiance to Jane Whaley, her doctrines and declarations. I know since I wore the badge for years. It was a costly choice.

The choice to *not* be required to celebrate any holiday seems antithetical when considering the Fourth of July. If there is one day that cherishes this country's freedoms, it is the Fourth of July.

Jane taught against fireworks. "Firecrackers were invented by the Chinese to scare off devils." No one should use fireworks. She did not allow her members to attend parades or other community activities. We were discouraged from reciting the Pledge of Allegiance.

The acknowledgment of this as a great country, combined with orders to not celebrate its formation and heritage confused me. WOFF gave a mixed message. The outside world is full of devils, yet we live in a great country. A conundrum. It can't be both ways. This nation is one of freedoms, opportunity and good folks, or all of those outside of WOFF are evil and ready to take our precious members to hell with them?

Which is it? While inside, I enjoyed certain freedoms. Yet, inside the group, Jane took away several freedoms in order to keep her kingdom going, growing and the money flowing.

Jane enjoyed more freedoms than regular members. She claimed, "That sin won't touch me, because it is not in me."

Her freedoms involved access to media, unlimited shopping trips (to secure God's blessings), and recreational and vacation activities. She enjoyed free access to resources beyond her admitted compensation. As regular members, we accepted the restraints she appeared unwilling to live by. Why did we proclaim to live in a free country when in fact we lived in the tightly controlled environment called Word of Faith Fellowship? I understand now we were deceived going in. In order to stay in the will of God, we chose to see what we needed to see, believe what we needed to believe, and ignore the rest which conflicted with our daily reality.

Easter

In the later years, we did not celebrate Easter. How did Jane rationalize that one? How does a Christian group convince their members to not celebrate a remembrance of events which are vital to the foundation of Christianity? As with other beliefs and practices, we evolved into this non-practice. To explain this one non-practice requires expounding on the entire subculture, as if in defense of it.

In addition, those who knew of my involvement asked, "How were you convinced not to celebrate Easter?"

The daily reality inside the group did not focus on *not* celebrating Easter or other restraints. WOFF life focused on Jane and whatever she wanted at that time, excused as her next revelation from God. Jane's perception became a member's ongoing reality.

If a faithful member questioned or rejected one or more parts of the evolving reality, they endangered the balance of their current known reality. They risked losing their family, job, house, circle of friends and so on. New recruits were not told this when they joined, but, accepting entrance into the group was viewed as a blanket acceptance of Jane's reality for herself, yourself, your family and any relationships you had while inside. Life in this group required submission of your total existence to the ever-changing, ever-evolving Jane-dictated rules, practices, and beliefs. Your life was truly not your own, it was the leader's. This commitment came under the guise of laying your life down for "the will of God."

In America, we have the freedom to not celebrate Easter, if we choose. Life inside skewed your ability to choose between your free-will desires and the group's desires as dictated by the leader. There was great peer pressure to conform to group practices if you wanted to stay. Rejecting a revelation for the group brings with it many negatives which must be navigated to continue living there.

How does a person who confesses the title of Christian not want to remember and celebrate the Resurrection of their Savior, Jesus Christ? Forget all the Easter bunny, eggs and candy, signs of early Druid worship. The central question remains, does remembering the hope that the Resurrection brings cause sin? The "sin" for members meant standing in the agreement with the world that celebrating the Resurrection should be contained to the one day. We were told the origin of Easter was in a celebration of an ancient fertility god. The mixture of terms and customs stemming from ancient pagan practices required members to abstain from the entire celebration. I was troubled with the term Easter before going into the group. I preferred making reference to the Resurrection as a reason to rejoice. That was my perception of what was important to me. By expressing my preference, I cast no stones or slight anyone their own beliefs.

This non-practice evolved alongside other changing dynamics which makes it difficult to segregate and give the explanation apart from the subculture itself. The understanding of the subculture is perplexing for those who have never lived inside because of the evolving interdependent dynamics.

Christmas

In years past, the church held special "Christmas Music Services" which later transitioned into "Special Music" services. Relatives and friends in the community were invited and attended in large numbers. After a time, the services were scheduled for two nights to accommodate the number of folks wanting to attend. However, over time, it became harder and harder to find Christmas songs that could stand the many tests of acceptability.

Jane's brother said, "Nowhere in the Bible does it say angels sing." This bit of information caused the exclusion of several songs. Since the service was an outreach, Jane wrote songs telling the story of Jesus' life from the gospels. These songs were quite lengthy.

Then, Jane realized demons surrounded birthdays. I was in the service when the news of the higher standard of God initially came forth. Jane stood at the front of the sanctuary walking around "getting ahold of the songs" for the Special Music service. She paused, time seemed to stand still. I felt a new revelation was about to be shared. After studying the floor for a time, she raised her head and grabbed a microphone. She explained the revelation from the Throne. She proclaimed Christmas as a birthday celebration for Jesus and celebrating it must be stopped. This revelation came to her a long time ago. She was just now able to share it with us.

Jane said, "God has dealt with me, and now He wants to deal with you."

This new dictate caused a thunderous uproar to say the least. Members were coached to write their relatives letters explaining the new understanding and why we no longer celebrated Christmas. This was a tense time as relatives became hostile, feeling rejected by us not attending the family Christmas gatherings.

I vividly remember a lunch in a restaurant with just my mother-in-law and me. She left no doubt as she pleaded with intensity for over an hour for my wife and me to reconsider this step of stopping Christmas celebrations. Though I heard her words, I could not agree as doing so would lead to worse drama in Spindale.

Many walk out strategies were formed. First, no presents; then presents received way before the season or after December 25th may be kept. Office parties for those still working for companies not owned by church members were a tricky deal. Even companies owned by church members with employees other than WOFF members had a sticky path to walk. What about Christmas bonuses or turkeys given out at Thanksgiving? Do you accept those gifts? If not, how do you refuse a bonus? It was such a confusing time. If you accepted the gift and were not supposed to, then you were "partaking of the table of demons!" according to Jane.

Somewhere during those years, my mom and step-father agreed to "meet us half-way." I don't recall if this meeting was before Christmas or after. We agreed to meet in Columbia, SC at the shopping center on Bush River Rd. There, while strangers strolled by, we exchanged gifts and hugs, smiles and politeness. Yes, I could tell there was a sincere strain on the relationship; however, in our clouded awareness, my wife and I considered it a victory to not have this meeting on Christmas, near a Christmas tree and all that goes with the holiday. We had kept the new restraints without polluting ourselves and our children. Now, I must ask, at what cost?

During a Sunday evening service, we were shown the *"Origins of Christmas"* video from the History Channel®. Children were told to cover their eyes and ears. Certain parts were fast-forwarded. From this video, the groundwork to reject Christmas and birthdays was laid in stone.

WOFF enjoyed several special meetings and seminars that focused on "the things of God." Why did we need holidays? We had week-long seminars in the month of May, during the week of Memorial Day. In July, we celebrated a youth seminar for all members. It occurred during the week of the Fourth of July. Next, there was the November seminar scheduled for the same week of Thanksgiving. The end of the seminar became a Fellowship Night.

The Apostle Paul wrote about certain convictions that needed to be kept personal and not taught as doctrine in the church.

Your personal convictions [on such matters]—exercise [them] as in God's presence, keeping them to yourself [striving only to know the truth and obey His will]. Blessed (happy, to be envied) is he who has no reason to judge himself for what he approves [who does not convict himself by what he chooses to do]. (Romans 14.22AMP)

After leaving WOFF, I learned many of Jane Whaley's personal convictions were taught as valid church doctrine. These "revelations" were tools of control.

CHAPTER SEVENTEEN

A CONUNDRUM...

For outsiders and for members, a conundrum existed around the fact that a few of this group's practices were similar with traditional Christian groups. It was hard for some to believe that a group which called themselves Christian and practiced basic ordinances of the Protestant church could be harmful to the members. This was the slippery slope which many, including myself, fell down while becoming entrapped in the web of WOFF.

Not all of the group's beliefs and practices were dangerous or unusual. Sustaining the membership would be impossible if no one benefitted from anything done or said. I do not deny that new members can and do receive benefits—at first. My experience proved one day the honeymoon ends and decisions must be made to continue paying the price of membership or paying the price to leave. Neither option was pleasant.

Let's review the normal practices. WOFF practiced certain rituals common to other Christian churches. From my years inside the group, I can safely say the following practices would be freely admitted by WOFF members. The list includes Baptism and Communion which are widely-accepted Christian practices. They would also list "Laying on of Hands," "Repentance" and "The Government of God." I understand the first two are common in the Protestant church. In many services, year after year, we heard teaching on the Government of God.

One noticeable omission might be the practice of foot washing. This was not talked about regularly. I remember participating in three foot washing services. The first one was more intense than the second or third. Though not practiced by several mainline or traditional Protestant churches, there is scriptural basis for the practice.

⁵After that, he poured water into a basin and began to wash his disciples' feet, drying them with the towel that was wrapped around him. ⁶He came to Simon Peter, who said to him, "Lord, are you going to wash my feet?" ⁷Jesus replied, "You do not realize now what I am doing, but later you will understand." ⁸"No," said Peter, "you shall never wash my feet." Jesus answered, "Unless I wash you, you have no part with me." ⁹"Then, Lord," Simon Peter replied, "not just my feet but my hands and my head as well!"
¹³"You call me 'Teacher' and 'Lord,' and rightly so, for that is what I am. ¹⁴Now that I, your Lord and Teacher, have washed your feet, you also should wash one another's feet. ¹⁵I have set you an example that you should do as I have done for you." (New International Version John 13:5-9, 13-15)

My memories are not very detailed regarding all three foot washing services. The first foot washing service was introduced with certain guidelines: men washing men's feet, women washing women's feet. Family members could wash each other's feet. The purpose was to humble yourself and make right any bitterness or unforgiveness with that person. Plastic basins were supplied with water. Towels were given for drying the feet. The service lasted several hours as there was a whole lot of washing to do. Many wept and from all indications, it mended several relationships. In these services, people filled the stage and used every available square foot of space not occupied by stacks of chairs, musical instruments or plants.

The second foot-washing service included a few more restrictions, and the service was shorter. I don't remember the exact modifications, but the same spirit was not in the second service as in the first. Maybe instead of sharing towels, we used paper towels? The children were allowed more freedom in the second service. The school classes participated in the services together.

By the third foot washing service, the water and basins were replaced with baby wipes and trash bags. The spiritual and emotional impact was reduced even further. I remember walking away thinking it had become ritual and not a "spiritual" practice. Baby wipes and trash bags. As with other things, you participated hoping for some experience, but in this case, I left still searching for answers as to what had happened and why.

Jane taught and practiced water baptism. In fact, I was baptized in the little pool behind the house at the end of the road past the church. Unless there have been major repairs, that pool is no longer used. The baptismal services were moved to Jane's house. Jane and Sam and chosen members of leadership baptized folks in the name of the Father, Son and Holy Ghost or Holy Spirit.

WOFF practiced communion. There was no certain time between communion services as in other church groups. It was whenever Jane "heard God to have communion." Sam and other leaders served the members. Children were allowed to partake if the parents allowed it. This observance was similar to communion services in other churches.

The elimination of cultural holidays and replacing them with WOFF-specific rituals and celebrations further cemented the members into the subculture while at the same time serving to separate them from their past, their non-WOFF families and outside friends. As with other practices, this dynamic was draped in Scripture references meant to shut off any dissent or individual choice or to exercise matters of conscience, molding members into an easily controlled group

CHAPTER EIGHTEEN

UNWRITTEN RULES

New members did not wait long before they were faced with new rules for daily living. These members were allowed more "grace" to learn, but soon they became as accountable to the long list of unwritten rules as older members. These unwritten rules were established by the leader.

The unwritten nature of the rules created mystique and power. Breaking an unwritten rule revealed a person's lack of spiritual maturity, lack of understanding of the things of God, or a hidden "devil." Suggesting that the person did not know the rule was too simple of an answer, even though these rules concerned the minutest detail of life inside the group. The rules were announced in open meetings or the school or your household.

Once Jane approved any new rule or code for conduct, the rule was LAW and breaking it was a sign of rebellion or laziness or some other devil. Any member breaking the rule may be publicly rebuked while the person pointing out the "sin" may be praised. Even if you missed the announcement during an open meeting, you were responsible for keeping the rule. This requirement made attendance crucial and asking members about a missed meeting vital. If you broke the new rule, saying "I did not know," this did not deflect your punishment.

Karel Reynolds often said to rule breakers, "Your heart should have been convicted to not do that... what sin were you giving to that kept you from hearing God?"

Thus, the great mystical power of the unwritten rules became evident to all and molded daily life. We accepted it as the "way God's people live." He knows all and Jane knows Him, so, Jane tells us what He says. It was never stated so plainly, but in reality, that was how we lived.

Service after service, seminar after seminar life inside the group was subject to "fine tuning" and revelation, so we could "walk in a higher place in God." Stopping the holidays, rules within households, rules or practices for relationships between family members or friends—all and more were defined by the ever-growing bevy of unwritten rules. Life inside was constantly reviewed for ways to "live closer to God." Who did not want that?

On the surface, certain rules did not seem bad. In fact, several pointed out safety issues. Each infraction may bring a public rebuke or a time of "being out of the church for your rebellion." The punishment could far outweigh the infraction, adding to the importance of keeping each rule and never forgetting them.

Does this sound like a happy place to live?

While inside, I admit being under "legalism." I remembered the exhortation in Colossians:

[20] If then you have died with Christ to material ways of looking at things *and* have escaped from the world's crude *and* elemental notions *and* teachings of externalism, why do you live as if you still belong to the world? [Why do you submit to rules *and* regulations?—such as]
[21] Do not handle [this], Do not taste [that], Do not even touch [them],
[22] Referring to things all of which perish with being used. To do this is to follow human precepts and doctrines.
[23] Such [practices] have indeed the outward appearance [that popularly passes] for wisdom, in promoting self-imposed rigor of devotion *and*

delight in self-humiliation *and* severity of discipline of the body, but they are of no value in checking the indulgence of the flesh (the lower nature). [Instead, they do not honor God but serve only to indulge the flesh.] (Col. 2:20-23 - AMP)

I knew that "legalism" was not a desired place for "someone walking with God."

How then did we accept all the many rules? I believe the sheer number of rules and reliance on obeying the rules gave us a sense of pride. They allowed us to see a definitive separation between us and the non-churched, including separation from others who called themselves Christian. The legalism affected us as it has other groups in the past. It puffed us up in pride. We were, in our eyes, the elite, the ones who were destined to make it to heaven if we submitted ourselves to God (through Jane). Is it possible the pride in the leader filtered down to her members?

How could we continue to accept more and more rules? We were exhorted to seek another level of submission, a higher place in God, and a place where sin could not touch us. In WOFF-lore, Jane lived as the only one "in that place where sin could not touch her." This level of holiness allowed her to have the televisions and free access to the media, all the clothes, the forty acre estate, the new cars, the best cell phones and the finest jewelry including a $24,000 diamond ring. She told us she lived "untouched by sin."

I think she believed every word of it. She believed she was above sin and had the authority to lead God's people as far as they could go in God. In her reality, no one could ever be as holy and free from sin as her. This was okay, since it meant her sinful members always needed her. She always had the ability to "hear God" and help her faithful members grow "closer" to a place they were never able to attain.

For the faithful who stayed year after year, it was hard to focus on the dynamics which pushed the system forward. There was a fog, created by the aura around Jane, preventing folks from seeing the real picture. This fog kept you off balance enough to believe the next load of religious cow manure being dumped from the podium. How could this be? How did members not see the stark reality of being soaked for "tithes and offerings" and fund raisers and robbed of sleep and relationships and basic free choices?

The number of rules expanded weekly, if not daily. Over time, some rules were replaced with a "higher way to walk" or became obsolete. When a rule changed, we were told "we don't do that anymore, God has shown us a better way." I never knew of anyone, myself included, who took time to count or write down the rules. Why do that? God brought them to you when you needed to know. Well, that did not always work and I don't think it was God's fault.

After I left in July of 2008, I listed all the rules I could remember. Below is a copy of my original list published on my blog. I first started posting about the "WOFF Don't" list in February of 2010. Some rules on this list are now obsolete.

WOFF Don't list

Don'ts – (this is a partial "living" list, at times, it takes on a life of its own, continuing to grow...)

1. Don't drink alcohol (includes beer, wine or liquor)
2. Don't cook with alcohol.
3. Don't eat at places that serve alcohol.
4. Don't drink root beer.
5. Don't drink Cheerwine®.
6. Don't drink diet Cheerwine®.
7. Don't drink ginger ale.
8. Don't smoke cigarettes.
9. Don't dip snuff.
10. Don't use chewing tobacco.
11. Don't associate willingly with those that do use tobacco.
12. Don't watch movies (unless Jane gives approval).

13. Don't watch videos in your cars.
14. Don't enter a movie theater (unless Jane gives approval).
15. Don't read newspapers not even the headlines.
16. Don't listen to the radio.
17. Don't read or handle magazines.
18. Don't watch television (except when allowed at church).
19. Don't read books that are not approved by leadership.
20. Don't read your Bible too much (Amplified version is acceptable).
21. Don't take notes during the services. Only record scripture references.
22. Don't forget to go to bathroom before the service.
23. Don't get up to go to bathroom during a service.
24. Don't bring knives of ANY type on church property.
25. Don't be late for a service or function.
26. Don't park alongside the left side of the sanctuary unless you are approved to do so.
27. Don't park in the spaces closest to the back steps. Those are reserved for parents with infants.
28. Don't park in the first spot along the front sidewalk. That is reserved for those on watch.
29. Don't park along the street. Use the field only when not raining.
30. Don't park on the drive to the school (unless approved for that service).
31. Don't park in the first handicap space unless approved.
32. Don't park under the awning and leave your car running.
33. Don't speed when driving around the church.
34. Don't go opposite to the accepted traffic flow of counter-clockwise. It causes confusion.
35. Don't be on your cell phone when approaching the school.
36. Don't drive your car with expired tags. You will be reminded.

37. Men: Don't wear a color of dress shirt except white or light blue.
38. Women: Don't get your heart set on a dress until you check with others to see if anyone else has that dress. You may need to return yours.
39. Don't "check out" during the singing.
40. Don't look around at others when you are supposed to be singing.
41. Don't close your eyes when singing. You could give over to a "religious devil."
42. Don't stare at visitors.
43. Don't bring your cell phone into a service. Exceptions are rare and you will be told when you can bring your phone into the service.
44. Don't take pictures during a regular service.
45. Don't make your own recording of a service.
46. Don't bring visitors unless you tell someone in the office so they can tell Jane.
47. Don't take pictures of Jane or other members unless you are given permission.
48. Don't be loose with your camera at any time.
49. Don't put large amounts of cash in the offering unless it is in an envelope.
50. Don't complain when the offering plates are passed more than once.
51. Don't allow your toddlers to eat in the sanctuary.
52. Don't bring snacks or dark drinks or chocolate.
53. Don't chew gum in the sanctuary.
54. Don't fall asleep during the services. If you get tired, take your Bible and stand up in the back of the sanctuary.
55. Don't wear muddy shoes or boots into the sanctuary, leave them at the door-outside.

56. Don't leave your tissues after services. Place them in the trash.
57. Don't leave coats, Bibles or personal belongings in the sanctuary. It gets locked after each service.
58. Don't touch the thermostats in the church unless you are approved.
59. Don't wear jeans (exception may be for construction work...maybe).
60. Don't wear shorts.
61. Don't wear sleeveless dresses or tops.
62. Don't wear dresses above the knees.
63. Don't wear a bathing suit without having it covered with long shorts (below the knees) and a dark t-shirt.
64. Don't wear cargo pants.
65. Don't wear or own anything with Nike® on it. Nothing.
66. Don't wear black tennis shoes.
67. Don't wear high-cut, boot-like tennis shoes.
68. Men: don't wear solid white tennis shoes.
69. Don't wear a baseball cap sideways or backwards.
70. Don't wear t-shirts with slogans or pictures.
71. Don't wear "muscle t-shirts."
72. Men: Don't leave the house without a white t-shirt on under your top shirt.
73. Don't go swimming with boys and girls together.
74. Don't leave the pool toys out when you are done using the pool.
75. Don't go outside without sunscreen (daily).
76. Men: Don't allow facial hair to grow. No beards, of any type. No "pork chop" sideburns.
77. Men: Don't let your hair get long or unkempt.
78. Don't interview for a job unless it is "under authority."
79. Don't accept a job unless you check it out with authority.

80. Don't make plans for college unless you have Jane check it out.
81. Don't sign-up for classes unless Jane Whaley or leadership checks out your schedule.
82. Don't buy a house unless Jane Whaley can check it out.
83. Don't even make an offer on a house unless Jane can "check out" and "get a feel" for the neighborhood.
84. Don't decorate your house unless Jane or her helper can help you.
85. Don't buy a car without checking with Sam first.
86. Don't sell a car or truck without checking with Sam first.
87. Don't get major repairs done without checking with Sam.
88. Don't buy insurance without checking with the approved church source person for insurance.
89. Don't plan a vacation or time away with your family unless you check it out with Jane.
90. Don't assume you can go to the funeral or a wedding of a family member without checking it out and/or someone from the church is going with you.
91. Don't celebrate Christmas.
92. Don't give gifts to others unless you are "under authority."
93. Don't celebrate Easter.
94. Don't celebrate other holidays.
95. Don't eat turkey on Thanksgiving.
96. Don't celebrate your birthday or others in your family or group of friends or co-workers.
97. Don't celebrate wedding anniversaries.
98. Don't go hunting.
99. Don't go fishing (well unless it is on an approved "ministry" trip).
100. Don't hunt or fish just for sport.
101. Don't have bumper stickers on your car (Political season is an exception).

102. Don't have "dingle dangles" hanging from your rearview mirror.
103. Don't have a slogan license plate on the front of your car.
104. Don't buy or drive a "race car" looking car.
105. Don't play games on your computer. Erase/delete the games.
106. Don't play games on your cell phone. Erase/delete them.
107. Don't own or use a "game boy" or other hand held electronic game device.
108. Don't play with regular playing cards.
109. Don't play hide and go seek.
110. Don't play Monopoly®.
111. Don't play football.
112. Don't ride in the back of a pick-up truck.
113. Don't play ping pong.
114. Don't play pool.
115. Don't play or imitate an "air guitar."
116. Don't play music without singing the words.
117. Don't whistle.
118. Don't let WOFF children play with children outside of WOFF.
119. Don't let children make animal sounds (maybe).
120. Don't let children play toy musical instruments (maybe).
121. Don't forget to read your Bible before you go to bed.
122. Don't let children play with camping toys.
123. Don't let children play with "play tools."
124. Don't let children have Bibles with stories and pictures of Jesus (maybe...).
125. Don't be late for anything. Be early.
126. Don't iron double creases in your pants.
127. Men: Don't use urinals that are not enclosed.
128. Don't store personal garments unless they are folded neatly in the drawer.
129. Don't go to tanning beds.

130. Don't ride motorcycles.
131. Don't ride ATV's or dirt bikes.
132. Men: African American- Don't shave your head bald.
133. Don't start a relationship without checking it out with Jane Whaley.
134. Don't decide who you will marry without checking it out with Jane.
135. Don't talk to the other person who you are in relationship with unless someone is listening and "guarding the conversation."
136. Don't talk loose and joke around. Don't be foolish.
137. Don't complain about the list of "don'ts."
138. Don't place the toilet paper on the roll unless it rolls over the top.
139. Don't speak to those who have left WOFF unless you ask Jane.
140. Don't ask anyone but Jane about those who lately have not been seen in services.
141. Don't go in the sanctuary with "sin in your heart," deal with it before service.
142. Don't expect someone else to clean-up your mess.
143. Don't back-talk or give excuses for your sin.
144. Don't "attack" those in authority.
145. Don't question Jane's authority to run WOFF.

Do you get the picture? As I reread the list, I remembered a few more rules and don'ts. This was the way we lived, there were always more rules and "don'ts" than you could remember in one sitting. Let's be clear, we were NOT told all the don'ts or rules before we joined. Do you think the number of recruits would go up or down if this list was shared with people before they decided to join?

There were several rules and "don'ts" which I left out at when I first recorded this list because I forgot them or was too embarrassed to

admit I had adhered to them. Now, I am more comfortable with my transition into WOFF and my exit. Let me add a few more don'ts.
We did not use cap-guns of any kind or snap-pops you threw on the ground. They were fireworks and that was a big no-no.

The introduction of cell phones and computers required more rules and more punitive measures for breaking the rules. We were told not to get on the Internet without a guard. Cell phones were not allowed for every WOFF member. I had one for business, but some members borrowed my phone because "God had not allowed them to have one." From recent survivor reports, mass distribution of information to members via text messages is the chosen method now. Yes, this adds another layer of mystique and responsibility to know what the text messages from the church office contain, as this might "save your life" or at least keep you from "coming under attack" by being somewhere or seeing something you were not allowed to see

CHAPTER NINETEEN

IF YOU DON'T LIKE IT, THERE IS THE DOOR

O n a more personal note, there was a period when we had to be "locked in" to know the right time to have intimate relations with our spouse. This lasted until a couple left and told the media. Soon after that happened, I was told we don't do that anymore. The change lasted for a couple of years. In 2007, we were told it was time to "go around that mountain again."

Brooke C. announced "If you don't like it—there is the door! We are going to have God's way in the marriage bed."

The classes for married couples started meeting again for instructions, confessions and rebukes regarding their "time in the marriage bed." The don't list for this activity included only using the accepted birth control- condoms. I never was required to get them from leadership, but some survivors told me two men in leadership bought condoms in bulk and sold or provided them to the husbands after they had "locked in." The only allowed position for God's people was missionary. There were practical instructions for limiting the noise since most couples lived in multi-family households. We were directed on a proper number of times per month and how to clean-up. Yes, folks, you read that.

If you go to church, are you required to ask leadership to have sex with your wife? Does your deacon supply you with condoms? Are you required to follow church approved rules in your bedroom? If you don't follow the rules, are you required to tell the person in authority over you about your "sin" and get prayer to be locked-in under authority? If you tell on your spouse, are they publicly rebuked in front of other church members about their sins in the marriage bed? Or, as in the case of Ken**, he suffered public rebuke for "taking care of himself" in the bathroom. Yes, folks, we had a meeting where the man was rebuked by his wife and church leadership for masturbating in his bathroom. I was in that meeting. I was in shock and disbelief. No children were present, but some of those meetings were taped so that Jane or others could "see what God was doing." Does this sound like legalism on steroids?

David Johnson and Jeff Van Vonderen share this insight in their book, "The Subtle Power of Spiritual Abuse":

"In abusive spiritual systems, people's lives are controlled from the outside by rules, spoken and unspoken. Unspoken rules are those that govern unhealthy churches or families but are not said out loud. Because they are not said out loud, you don't find out that they're there until you break them....

*When you find unspoken rules by breaking them unintentionally, you will suffer one of two consequences: either **neglect** (being ignored, overlooked, shunned) or **aggressive legalism** (questioned, openly censored, asked to leave—in extreme cases cursed)."* [6]

CHAPTER TWENTY

ESSENTIAL BELIEFS

In order to sustain this extensive, legalistic, control system, there were elemental notions required for members to embrace. I lived under the three unspoken and unwritten rules below for years, even if I did not gladly admit them.

The main unwritten, unspoken rule: *Members were required to live life as if Jane Whaley was the ONLY true source of the knowledge of God or God's will.*

All of life inside this group rests on this unspoken foundation. This foundation gives power to the legalism. If there was another source who could enact or approve rules, there would be confusion.

What starts as a simple question to a new person: "Did you check that out with someone leadership?" grows into a requirement to check out all of your life decisions with Jane. Over the years, I "locked in" with a minister who then conferred with Jane. During my WOFF days, I had few times of personal contact with Jane. However, she did send decisions through someone else which affected my life. This dynamic was a great source of angst and bewilderment for me. Why did I have to ask a person if what I am about to do is okay?

Have you ever seen the Wizard of Oz? It had the same feel to it: "Don't pay any attention to the guy (gal) behind the curtain!" But I lived it and did so for many years. I cannot deny, at least to some degree, I accepted this foundational deception. I lived as if Jane

Whaley's ability to hear God was vital to walking with God and being a Christian. In reality, it was only vital to walking and living in WOFF.

Toto, I don't think we are in Kansas anymore.

From this unspoken rule stems two others: *If Jane predicted it and things happened the way she predicted, then for sure it was God's will.*

Do I need to elaborate? I was under this deception for years. Fact: not everything Jane predicted came true. When things did not take place the way Jane predicted, then the predictions were glossed over or buried under the next unfolding drama.

The next unwritten rule: *If Jane does it, it must be right, if Jane said it, it must be God.*

How can folks live under this? It was a gradual submission for some. I lived under it and only a few times expressed any doubt. I believed first and doubted later...a practice which cost me, dearly.

You may ask how someone can know that certain things are not "normal" in the Body of Christ and yet continue to do them regardless of the criticism. I did not consider WOFF life and all the resulting stares from outsiders as an indictment against my personal faith. Therefore, I did not see the criticisms of Jane Whaley and the group as personal attacks.

Was this thinking in itself evidence of deception? How can someone be a part of a group for years and think the criticisms of the group do not reflect on them? Simply put, I was deceived and lived under the legalism.

Legalism of this type also requires a caste system. While a member, I lived in, and endorsed by my participation, the WOFF caste system. At the top sat Jane Whaley above everyone. Next, there was a core group of Jane's family and certain ones who were followers from the group's early years in Tulsa. Ones in this group made decisions and were in regular contact with Jane. The next level was leadership. This group was given responsibilities and experienced more freedoms than regular members. Inside this leadership group there were different levels. Some were leadership for years, others ebbed and flowed in and out of this level depending on the sin they manifested. Jane determined who lived at each level in her caste system.

Lastly, the largest group, at the bottom of the pyramid, was the regular members. These members did the work, gave their time, sang the songs and did whatever was needed to "fulfill their call." These folks Jane called "full of sin" and were at any time "on their way out" for any infraction. I was a regular member. I talked to someone else in leadership in order to obtain "wisdom" and answers from Jane. This system allowed the concentrated power of the group to flow from the top, Jane Whaley. Through this caste system, members were hurt and misled. The function of this system allowed the controls set in place to seem mystical and spiritual.

During the early years of WOFF, Jane and Sam Whaley called themselves Apostles. I had no personal experience with a minister being officially called an Apostle. Why did I not see this as a sign something was amiss? I did not raise a question about it. Of course, a person can call themselves whatever they want, but I said nothing. From my actions, I appeared as if I believed and agreed with it. I regret participating in this system and the legalism that flowed through it. Amidst the legalism, we had a schedule to keep and a life to be lived.

CHAPTER TWENTY-ONE

A TYPICAL WEEK

The life routine of each faithful member revolved around the happenings at the church. If you had school-aged children, your life revolved around the school schedule. Parents were responsible for transporting students to and from school. You were required to help them with their homework and any projects. Planning "time away" for your family depended on the school schedule. We did not use the term vacation. Who takes a vacation from God?

If you did not have children, your schedule revolved around your ministry opportunities at the church. Anyone unemployed might be asked to help on work projects in members' homes or with projects at the church. Retired members were locked in to look after someone in need. This could include bringing them to daily prayer or taking them to doctor's appointments.

The school met five days a week and generally followed the Rutherford County school system schedule. Jane Whaley was the principal of the school, and if she "heard God" to change the schedule, it changed. After her grandson was born, she started teaching in the school. Jane became a very hands-on teacher to no one's surprise.

Sunday church services normally began at 9:00AM for prayer and service at 9:30AM. The morning services lasted longer in the earlier days. By 2008, we finished around noon. After morning services, there may be meetings or a bake sale or another fund raiser in the fellowship hall. After each service, different households were required to stay after services to clean the sanctuary, bathrooms and office building.

Sunday evenings started at 6:00PM for prayer and service at 6:30PM. In the 1990s, Sunday evening services lasted longer. By 2008, Jane usually finished the preaching and the announcements before 9:00PM. Parents were told to get those children home to bed. If you delayed for no good reason, you might be subject to a scolding for staying around too long.

Prayer before the services was in the fellowship hall. During this thirty minute period, blasting and deliverance was common for members "under attack." If the lights blinked on and off, then we stopped praying. We stopped blasting because an unlearned person approached, and they would not understand our revelation. They might "come under attack."

After Sunday evening service, there were meetings of different types. Members seeking time with Jane or someone in leadership lined up outside of Jane's office door before and after services. These members came to lock-in and admit a sin or to tell of someone else's sin or to lock-in about a decision: whether to take a trip, which clothes to wear or make-up or hairdo, or what job or class to take. WOFF legalism required a lot of locking in and making sure Jane had "ahold of your life." Did we members understand by locking in about every little thing, we were being locked-in, in more ways than one? We were giving away our responsibility to think for ourselves and have an individual relationship with Him. Jane became our high priestess. We were told "locking in" was how God's people walked in holy righteous living.

Wednesday evenings started at 6:30PM for prayer and service at 7:00PM, with the same routine of prayer in the fellowship hall-- blasting and deliverance. The Church service may be more informal or not. If visitors were in any service, that service contained a lot of singing... *To the Nations!* or *I will fulfill My Call...* song after song. We sang the songs Jane wrote.

Group after group, arranged however Jane desired to display her trophies, walked to the stage to sing. Children were grouped by ages. Some sang solos- if they were "taking hold." Men, College Age, Young Marrieds, Older Singles everyone was subject to being called upon to sing. Years earlier, Jane taught us how important it was to smile, open your mouth, sing loud and jump on cue.

Many times during visitor services, testimonies from the youth followed the singing. Visitors rarely witnessed the "family meetings" where people were rebuked for sin. The family meetings were saved for the regular members and those who Jane knew, by the Spirit of God, could take hold to watch how God dealt with His people. Most Friday nights, there were fellowship and fund-raising dinners. After eating, children played, and adults watched children. Singles fellowshipped with someone of the opposite sex after locking in to make sure they were hearing God. Clean-up after fellowship dinners lasted until 10:00PM or after.

Any night of the week you could be asked to help with a work project. Any day of the week, your schedule might include helping someone move. When God said someone had to move, it happened quickly, many times on the same day. Scads of folks descended on your house with trucks, boxes and hands ready to move you to your next household. Of course, Jane had the final say as to who lived with whom.

Members' schedules regularly included a shift on overnight watch at the church. First shift started at 10:00PM and ended at 2:45AM. The second crew watched until 7:00AM. Many times watchers left early to be on time for their jobs. The time between 6:00AM and 7:00AM – might be uncovered. The first church office worker showed up around 7:45AM. There were some nights when second shift was not covered.

Filling the slots for watch times was quite a deal. Before and after Sunday evening service, the person tasked with this chore arrived at the podium. Men looked down, squirmed in their chair, or left for the bathroom. This weekly drama became confrontational depending on the skill of the slot filler. Soon, the pleas turned to one-on-one questions with individuals being called out to volunteer.

"When did you last do watch?"

"Why can't you do watch this week?"

"Do you know this is the will of God?"

Some men never did watch, for whatever reason. Maybe they were too far up the pyramid structure. All of the scheduling struggles ended when Jane stood up to assist the name taker. She had the touch. Suddenly, forgetting sleep, laying down your life for four hours in the middle of the night was the easiest thing on earth. Imagine that.

I started volunteering for watch in 2002. At the time, the second shift was required to sleep in the school building. There were mats or mattresses available to move into a classroom. It was hard sleeping in the school which made for a long second shift. Over time, people were allowed to go home and sleep before second shift. Years later, married couples were allowed to do watch together. This option meant adult conversation. WOFF life did not provide much time for relaxed conversation with adults, including talking with your spouse. Later, watch time slots were filled with two ladies.

I saw many strange things on watch. I saw deer, foxes, skunks and opossums, and, yes, at most any hour some folks drove down Old Flynn Road shouting out the windows, screaming, spinning tires, playing loud music and blowing horns. It was usually young folks out for a joy ride. Some looked lost, turning around at the end of the road. No matter why non-members drove on Old Flynn Road, the watchers tried to record the license plate number.

The next day, this information, including a narrative, was given to a particular church secretary. Plate numbers were run for identification. How they acquired access to that information, I am not sure. But, the church's private detective knew the license plate information as well as who had been in the car. That was his ministry.

A few men talked freely during watch, things you never heard during the day. One man always told me his thoughts on sensitive issues. This kept things cooking and before you knew the shift was over. Conversations at such an hour were informative.

Living inside WOFF consumed your life. At any moment, on any given day, your plans were subject to change. A call from leadership redirected you into "the will of God." Who wanted to be out of "the will of God?" If you balked, you were subject to correction and rebuke. Your life was never your own until you took it back by leaving.

PART THREE

DECEMBER 2002

CHAPTER TWENTY-TWO

LIFE CHANGING EVENTS

I started part-time with Two Mile Properties (TMP) in December of 2002. For the first few days, I acted as a taxi driver for other workers without transportation. Additionally, I painted and helped move supplies to the right work site. Within a few weeks, I received the papers, cell phone and a small box of keys which added the management of local rental properties to my list of tasks. By then, my job was full time.

The Credit Union job in Greenville ended while the work in Rutherford County exploded. A total of five telephone numbers were forwarded into my cell phone. The phone rang constantly with folks responding to newspaper ads, wanting to look at rental property and tenants reporting repair issues and vendors.

In a moment of desperation, I told Linda Southerland that the phone rang constantly.

I lamented, "Some days I want to get in a corner and cry."

She scoffed, "This is good for you, (and) it is preparing you for the ministry!"

I had a hard time understanding how answering the phone constantly six and seven days a week helped me be a minister. No, thank you. This impractical solution did not last long. The local rental property duties were soon given to another member in the church.

Next, Two Mile Properties purchased an apartment complex in Gaffney. I was given the rental manager duties. In 2003, I began working there even though I knew very little about the management of apartments. While talking to a manager of another complex, the subject of licensing came up. He was shocked I was given the job and not told I needed to be licensed. Josh Farmer was a real estate broker, and he thought I could work under his license for a while. Soon thereafter, I took real estate classes.

Long hours, steep learning curves, mistakes and drama, these described the first year of my life working in Gaffney. The residents were warm and friendly folks. I met a couple of young men, who were brothers, and took them to special church meetings. I thought I was helping them at the time, but it was awkward. Not as awkward as managing the apartment pool. I took certification classes to monitor the pool chemicals. Knowing the group rules, consider the contortions I went through to avoid giving over to the devil while checking the chemical levels when the pool was occupied. I considered it part of the job. I did not discuss it with anyone in the church.

Despite my inexperience in managing apartments, I collected rent. My experience in the local magistrate courts helped when evictions were filed. My learning curve mainly fell in the areas of ordering supplies, planning maintenance and learning the Fair Housing rules.

In January 2004, the owners of TMP bought another apartment complex in Spartanburg. I moved to the manager's position at Timbercreek Apartments. This was farther away from home and required a different level of management. I needed all I had learned in Gaffney and more. There was a pool, and I underwent many of the same antics to check the chemicals and not get accused of "giving over to lust" while doing my job. There were renovations to the pool performed by a church-member-owned construction company.

The entire complex was being renovated, adding to the stress of trying to collect rent while renting out the finished apartments. My immediate supervisor, Andy K. and another church member, serving as director of renovations and maintenance, moved into the apartment office. The second fellow was qualified to do the maintenance job. The rest of us learned through on the job training.

Prospective tenants and residents did not know the legalism we lived under. Many times, I had to ignore their infractions to our rules and go on as if nothing ever happened.

In October of 2004, I felt some chest pains during the praise and worship part of the church services. We were expected to jump up and down "with our whole heart" while singing. It was an intense aerobic session. At first, I thought it might be a previous medical issue flaring up in my esophagus. But, it continued, and I stopped jumping. By the middle of November, I noticed the pains while climbing the stairs to second floor apartments. One day, I casually mentioned this to Andy K. His response was to slough it off and laugh at my pains, drawing in the other guy in the office. I did not appreciate his mockery but did not make a big deal of it. There were other matters to consider.

November meant the seminar and next came the Christmas avoidance season. The children were released from classes during late December. The task of not celebrating and deciding how or when to go see relatives was at hand. By then, we avoided contact with relatives during December. It was much easier this way. My wife and I took first watch on Wednesday, December 29th. We planned to use this time to talk and catch-up with each other.

During our shift, we walked around the church to stay awake. It was a cold night; I was ahead of her going up the hill by the sanctuary. I felt pains in my chest, and I climbed into the van and started the heater, breathing in the warm air. The pains subsided, and I took the relief as a sign this pain was no big deal. Later, I walked around the church and experienced the same pain relieved by the same warm air in the van. When our relief crew showed up, we went home to bed.

The next day, I faxed my doctor a short version of the events from the previous night. Within minutes, he was on the phone asking some probing questions. After this brief exchange, he said I needed a stress test and that this could be serious. It was too late to get a test done that day, and his office was closed the next day. He warned me if there were any more symptoms over the weekend, to not go to the local hospital but go to a hospital a few miles away. Monday, I was scheduled for a stress test.

On January 3, 2005 at 1:00PM, I arrived at his office in the company van. My wife met me. Sure, I was concerned but had no idea what events were about to unfold. In high school, I ran on a treadmill for a stress test as part of the research for a local university. Those results were excellent. I was familiar with the process.

This day was different. After a minute and a half, the doctor stopped the test. He told me to get dressed and wait in his office with my wife. I was confused since I did not feel any pain before he stopped the test.

After a few minutes, the doctor entered, his smile replaced with a look of concern.

"You have a problem on the back right-hand side of your heart. You are a candidate for a major event. I made some calls to Mission Hospital. They are waiting for you at the ER. They will do a heart catheterization to learn more. You are not to drive. Martha will drive... Do you have any questions?"

He reiterated, "You are not to drive. Martha will drive to the hospital."

"Can we get something to eat on the way?"

"Be sure it is healthy," he answered.

After gathering my belongings and making some calls, we were on our way to Asheville. It was a solemn ride, but what was there to say? We were stunned. Heart problems were new to me. We called someone to care for the children and for a co-worker to pick-up the company van. Our lunch choice was a fried chicken sandwich. We had a lot to learn.

We entered the emergency room and were met by a team of hospital personnel. After assigning us a space, Dr. Wayne* came in to do an interview and assess my condition. He went through some basic questions. During this interview, I let him know my requests.

"I do not want any music during the procedure or any form of Versed®.

These were both church-prompted requirements.

He eyes widened, "Will you take a blood transfusion?"

"Yes," I replied. *No, I am not a Jehovah Witness.*

He was visibly relieved.

By this time, it was late in the afternoon. My procedure was scheduled for 9:00AM the next morning. I admit I was anxious. The new sights, sounds and smells made the whole experience frightening. My wife stayed overnight with me. During the night, the nurse woke me. The doctor entered the room.

He said, "You have had a minor heart episode. It is good you are here. Rest now."

"Yes, thank you."

I had grown used to the pain and did not know how serious my health issues were.

The next day Gerald and Linda Southerland visited us. My time for the heart catheterization kept getting pushed back by cases more serious than mine. This procedure required fasting, and the small talk was not feeding my stomach. Finally, my turn came, and I was moved back to the waiting area at 3:00PM. While I waited, a male nurse came to me and told me God had told him to pray for me. He cut loose right there in the hallway. It was kind, but awkward, for a non-member to pray for me. I needed it. His prayer was simple and brought comfort. I had no idea what lay ahead for me on the other side of those swinging doors.

The moment came, and I was wheeled in to a room full of strange equipment and electronic sounds creating a sea of new stimuli. I tried to relax and field the questions which were meant to keep me engaged. I had requested to be awake and able to view the monitors during the procedure.

Dr. Montana* performed the procedure. He admitted being perplexed since he was not allowed to have his music during the operation. He grudgingly agreed to the requirements and acknowledged he knew my referring physician.

"You are too young to be on my table," he said.

"Yes," I agreed. *That made me feel no better. I was only 43.*

I will never forget the images which flashed on the monitor screen. Those images changed my life. I had a severe blockage on the back right-hand side of my heart and three other minor blockages. He performed angioplasty and inserted a stent. I felt immediate relief. My life has never been the same since that day.

Recovery included a gradual acclimation to a rehab routine. I did not return to work for a week. During the recovery time, the Farmers transferred me back to Gaffney where the stress level was less. This move helped in many ways.

My diet had to change and my wife was on board. She did whatever was needed to accommodate my new food choices. I started walking the hall of the school a few minutes at a time. This was all tenuous, but necessary to gain a new level of health. My son, who was ten years old, accompanied me for some of the walking. I appreciated his company and loving support.

After a couple of weeks, I began rehab at a facility in Spartanburg. The care was excellent and the routines were continuously monitored. It was difficult to get there in the mornings, but Josh Farmer allowed me to be late in order to participate in the workouts. A Gaffney resident was taking rehab at the same time and we attended together on many mornings. During this time, I learned how far from good health I lived. Exercise and diet changes helped me lose over 30 pounds.

At the end of January, I took another stress test and passed. The doctor cleared me for a church-sponsored trip to Brazil. What a relief. His approval helped me gain the needed confidence to travel to a foreign country just a few weeks after major surgery.

CHAPTER TWENTY-THREE

MY BRAZIL TRIP
FEBRUARY 2005

Several months before the heart attack, I signed up for the Brazil trip in early February. By January, the ticket was paid for, and the detailed preparations began. I was glad to be able to go on this six day trip. A trip out of the country was a rite of passage, another badge of honor. The trip to Brazil was exciting not only for me, but for my family and close friends. *"God has seen fit to provide the finances and the place in the spirit for you to go. You must have had big breakthroughs and have been taking hold and staying locked-in!"*

Since our first arrival in Greenville, I had heard wonderful stories about the Brazil trips. The stories included the "fight to get everyone on the right plane."

Jane's story about her briefcase being stolen from her car while stopped at a red light was a classic. The door to their car was unexpectedly opened by a stranger who grabbed the briefcase. Suddenly, Jane popped out of the car and ran down the sidewalk with Brooke not far behind. Can you imagine? Jane and Brooke chasing the thieves in their high heeled shoes, or maybe Jane was barefoot? I can't remember it all. The story ended with a young street boy diving into a canal to rescue the briefcase carrying all the group's passports.

Jane told stories about the arguments at the ticket counters of different airports, in different countries. She exclaimed she went "toe to toe" with the ticket clerk and the manager. All of this was of course to ensure that all WOFF travelers were on the right plane, which meant all on the same plane. Over the years, this requirement changed to allow two or more groups to travel on different planes.

Church trips to Brazil were no small undertaking. Over one hundred folks gathered together and either boarded one plane or divided up into a few different flights. The days leading up to the trip to the airport were busy with completing forms, getting your list of things to pack and of course packing what you could to stay under the suitcase weight limit. In the fellowship hall, we arranged the chairs like the airplane seats, and we practiced boarding and exiting the plane.

We were schooled in airplane etiquette for ministers. The main rule was keeping your head and eyes down while the movie played. You were instructed how to guard yourself from "those not walking with God." For safety concerns, many of the grouping measures were beneficial. We were never alone while traveling.

Selecting the right things to pack took some forethought. There was no guessing. Members don't "guess." If you could not hear God on what to take, ask someone who had been. Many times, this trip required new clothes. You must have "clothes to match the gift of God in you."

Details were decided ahead of time. You paid bus money, airport taxes, food money and other fees. Nothing was left to chance or the "devil could attack." Some measures covered how to ensure ladies did not end up beside a stranger who could "attack them with lust." Of course, you knew not to look at the magazines in the plane. A few members packed blinders, for sleeping of course.

By 2007, the airport regulations had increased concerning what to pack and how to pack. These rules were stressed over and over. Even among the pressures of preparation, it was all exciting. I had flown before but never out of the country.

The day for departure arrived; the caravan was arranged. Everyone was "locked-in" with someone. In this case, we used a buddy system and made arrangements assist those who needed help carrying their luggage. All drivers tried to keep their cars together on the way to the Charlotte airport. There was tangible excitement as folks hugged loved ones and said their goodbyes. We gathered into the waiting area, and there the love kept coming.

As we entered the Charlotte airport lobby area, all of us moved over to the right facing the escalators. We waited there with our carry-on bags, talking nervously, trying to take hold of our minds and not give over to some kind of devil. I stood near a young man, Tim*, who I was only vaguely familiar with. We were locked in and told to sit next to each another on the flight.

Jayne Caulder stood close to us. She was not making this trip, but came to the airport as a "guard." I overheard her get Tim's attention. "Why do you have double creases in your pants? You know we don't do that. You weren't taking hold!"

She did not wait for a reply. Her gift was to explain in great detail how to avoid double creases the next time he ironed his pants.

Tim meekly took his correction and replied, "Yes."

Jayne loved everyone with that kind of gift. She showed little awareness of this young man's struggles in finding the courage to go to Brazil. To her, having double creases was an abomination. It was an attack on the move of God. After listening to her "love" on Tim, I knew I had no regrets about her staying in North Carolina. Little did I know what waited for me in the coming days.

We changed planes in Atlanta. The temperature was near thirty-two degrees and rainy. Ice formed on the plane; however, we took off flying direct to Sao Paulo, Brazil on an overnight flight. I did not sleep much. We landed and exited the plane walking into a hallway, waiting to be checked through.

My first memories include standing in a warm hallway with announcements only in Portuguese. It was soon very apparent air-conditioning was a rare luxury in Brazil. I felt strange in a place where English was not the main language. We made it through customs and found several folks from the host church waiting to load our baggage. The familiar faces were a welcome sight in this bustling, strange, new environment.

We boarded buses to our destination, Franco de Roca, where the host church was located several miles outside of the city. Our ride took us through several bad areas, so the curtains were shut to "keep out the unclean." Several folks slept during the trip. I sat in the back of the bus grateful for the air-conditioning. I did not know when or where I would get any rest that day.

After a long and bumpy ride, we arrived in the area of the church. We pulled up to a large house and got off the bus to walk and stretch our legs. This large house sat on a crest of a hill, a home for a wealthy family. The owners were a couple in the church. The husband owned a factory in another city. This large house was not their primary residence. During the seminar, about thirty-five women and girls stayed there.

As I look back on this trip, my memories include visions of the Brazilian people as gracious, loving and accommodating. They opened up their homes for over one hundred Americans to stay for several days. This large number of visitors stressed their water supplies as well as their waste disposal systems. What ever happened, the people kept a good attitude, smiled big and proved to be more than kind to us. I have fond memories of my time with them, learning, taking in their lifestyle and surroundings. Meeting the Brazilians and experiencing their sincerity was very enjoyable.

After stopping at the first house, we rode down the hill around to the main entrance of the church. The luggage was unloaded. We were grouped by the assigned household list and ferried to our respective homes to settle in. We were in a neighborhood on a large hillside. I noticed between the large expensive gated homes, the streets were gravel. I was told "because of the poverty," everyone needed heavy security for their properties.

Our group of about thirty members stayed in a large impressive home on three acres. The surrounding fence was brick with large electric wooden gates. The owners were a sweet couple who served as leadership in the local church. Their estate included a large home, a pool and a large pool house. Another family lived in the pool house. Grouped in different locations were various fruit trees, some near the front and others at the back of the property.

The owners had three guard dogs, two of which were German Shepherds. These large dogs took commands in three languages: Portuguese, English and German. Each guest allowed the dogs to greet them and sniff them. During this greeting, a young man became frightened and a dog jumped on him, growling. He showed more fear and this became quite an incident. After a minute or two, the owner calmed the dogs, and the young man regained his composure. The young man was instructed to not show fear. I overheard someone say he was not "taking hold." I knew it was more complicated than this trite phrase allowed.

After we unpacked, we were shown around the property. There was plenty of living space and a large kitchen. The spacious bathrooms had large, tiled showers. I remember large closets and a beautiful courtyard. The young men stayed in bunk beds in a large room on the top floor. I slept on the top bunk near a door to a balcony. There was no central air, but the nights were comfortable in the 70s with a breeze through the open doors. Kent Covington stayed upstairs with the men and young boys. Brooke Covington stayed downstairs with the women and girls.

We ate breakfast in the houses and lunch and dinner at the church. Feeding the Americans took planning and lots of help. Many church members labored for hours to cook, serve and clean-up after each meal. Every effort was made to accommodate the Americans with menu choices. This church kept a snack bar open after meetings with drinks, candy and ice cream for sale. We were told not to drink the tap water unless it was filtered.

We arrived on a Thursday morning and left on Monday morning. The first night, we attended a meeting at the church for the Americans. It was not safe to walk the streets, so we were driven to the church. At this meeting, schedules and guidelines were explained as well as a warning about the dogs from the previous incident. Strategies and plans were laid out for the Americans to be involved in the ministry during and after the meetings on Friday and Saturday and help before and after the wedding on Sunday night.

A Brazilian couple was getting married with Jane presiding over the ceremony. This was standard for weddings in America and in the WOFF-related churches. If Jane did not do the ceremony, then the couple did not get married.

We also covered who "had it" to speak and what to say. Everyone was required to "*find someone to take hold of.*" This was not a vacation. We were encouraged to get as much rest as possible because there was plenty of work to do before the wedding. We also knew the seminar meetings ran long on Friday and Saturday.

The service was translated from English. I recognized the music as the same we heard in North Carolina, so I could figure out the words to the songs which were in Portuguese.

Friday and Saturday filled up with morning and evening meetings, ministry, meals and then more ministry. Sleep was optional. The evening conversations included planning the bathroom schedule and learning about the seminar schedule for the next day.

During one meeting, I helped in a classroom for kindergarten or first grade. The class leaders told the children to sit-up straight and fold their hands on their desk. The services were broadcast from the sanctuary by closed circuit to the classrooms. Each class followed along with the singing, preaching and praying. Obeying the rules was difficult for some children, so they were escorted out for "help." Many returned taking their seat with a renewed submission. During one of these meetings, I was the only one who spoke English. This was difficult, but fun. I felt like an observer and now understanding the idolatry which existed, it saddens me that others looked to me as special.

Before one of the services, while I was sitting in the sanctuary talking to another member from North Carolina, Kent came and rebuked us. "This is no vacation. Go take hold of someone!"

Suddenly, the WOFF tape played in my head, *"You will never find your place in God until you help someone else find their place in God."* Never mind your issues (devils) – "go help someone else get their devils out and your issues will fade."

I had heard this line a few hundred times. Both of us got up and found some teenage boys who looked like someone should "take hold of them." This meant they were off by themselves with no adults.

Ministry looked like zone defense at times. Spread out and do something WOFF-like. Look good in your clothes, smile and point out when someone gave to unclean, stopped paying attention or broke a rule. We were encouraged to ignore our problems and go help others. Help translated in repeating to them the words, scriptures, mantras we heard in North Carolina. We were making disciples of them from what we were taught from Jane and other leadership. I did not understand this dynamic until years later.

We did not trade pictures or gifts with folks from other churches. Years before, Jane stopped this practice. If you wanted to contact someone after you met them in Brazil, all of that communication was cleared through the church office in North Carolina. So, the time for ministry and meeting the local members happened during the seminar. Each service included time for prayer and deliverance after the preaching. We judged if a meeting went well by the length of the prayer, blasting and deliverance times afterwards. Both churches used this as a gauge.

"Wasn't that a good meeting last night? We prayed for *two hours* AFTER Jane stopped teaching. Whew, I was blessed...Did you get prayer? I got deliverance."

Every day was packed with group activities. From the time our feet hit the floor until we closed our Bible at night, we were on stage. We watched each other do everything. If someone gave to sin and you saw it, you were compelled to tell someone. If you did not, you had "it" in you. We were WOFF members doing WOFF things; only we were in a different country. I did not realize it then, but the net effect of these seminars was to teach Brazilians the WOFF ways. These folks were hungry to be like WOFF in North Carolina.

I compare this to the idolatry and the feelings of being in the Greenville church prior to 2002. In Greenville, there was the unspoken, understood notion that WOFF members in North Carolina were living in God's will. You were to learn from them and want to be like them. I lived in this idolatry while in Greenville. This is obvious; otherwise, I wouldn't have spent thousands of dollars in gas and all those hours of traveling back and forth to Spindale.

When I moved to Spindale, I recognized the dangers of this idolatry. Many of the Brazilians were infected with the same idolatry and unfounded envy for the Americans. Did the idolatry serve a good purpose? I do not believe so. In my opinion, it puffed up the Americans and deceived the Brazilians. Jane and her members, me included, lead these folks down an empty road. The rules and endless laws we brought offered no lasting heart changes. When I walked among the Brazilian people, they dressed like WOFF members; they emulated Jane Whaley, North Carolina leadership and regular members. Jane Whaley and her members exported WOFFness to Brazil.

Though the meetings during Friday and Saturday were important, all of the focus soon concentrated on the weeding at hand. Sunday was very warm and very busy, each minute packed with a variety of duties. It was a blur. There was a church service in the morning, afterwards lunch at the church. After this, the preparation for the wedding moved into high gear. All afternoon, there were things to do and people to help. I worked in one of the kitchens chopping fruit until the wedding started. The only place for me to change clothes was the school office. Quickly! When I finished, I stuffed my work clothes in a cabinet drawer and opened the door acting as if it was perfectly normal to change clothes in an office.

The sanctuary was packed to overflowing. I stood in the back leaning against the wall. During the ceremony, I almost passed out from the heat. The fellow next to me steadied me a couple of times. It was very warm in the sanctuary, though the fans were blowing. After the wedding and clean-up, we returned back to the estate.

We finished our time in Brazil and made our way home, leaving on Monday and traveling overnight. We arrived back in Charlotte during the early afternoon on Tuesday. After stopping for lunch near the airport, we returned to the church. There we walked in to an extended prayer meeting. Jane's latest court drama fueled the hours of loud prayer. I was so hyped; I stood in the front of the sanctuary and helped lead. I was glad to go and glad to be back in America. The Brazilian people still hold a special place in my heart; however, I have regretted taking the WOFF ways to them.

CHAPTER TWENTY-FOUR

RETURN TO NORTH CAROLINA

Upon returning to North Carolina in February, my altered, healthier routine lasted a few months. After finishing the cardiac rehab sessions in Spartanburg, I merged back into the normal work and church routine. I thought there was less stress, but how was I to accurately measure the level of stress if I only measured it against the levels during the last months leading up to the heart attack? I came close to dying from the combination of factors during that time, why compare my life to any other months?

Sadly, this trap keeps many folks in WOFF. They only compare the present drama to the one previous, thinking the new one was not that bad. This incremental acclimation to more and more strenuous and absurd requirements trapped many in WOFF. Church members had no safe reality available for comparison.

The daily work/church routine began eating deeper into my time with my family. Other than occasional family outings, more days than not, I worked long hours and went to church. By August of 2005, I grew more dissatisfied. One Friday night, instead of attending the fellowship dinner or spending time with my family; I stayed in Gaffney preparing an apartment for a Saturday move-in. Another member stayed to help. My wife learned I was again working late; she drove the children to have dinner with me. We ate in the van while parked at the apartment complex. As they drove off, I lost my willingness to continue the charade. I determined to make changes.

That next week, I found an opening at a Credit Union where I had previously worked for ten years. After driving to visit with the Credit Union president, I made an offer for services that was accepted. The initial contract was only for a few months. While driving back and forth from that interview, the previous drama scenes played in my head. Louder still were the desires to stop working in the Two Mile Properties machine. I did not expect my wife to agree to the changes. But, I did not want to keep on the way things were.

The expected backlash came as I announced the changes to my wife and then to leadership. I knew it was coming, but it did not matter. Over the few next weeks, I trained another person from the church for the job in Gaffney. By October, I finished training the new manager, then, I only worked for two Credit Unions, one in Marion and one in South Carolina. This work was stress-free compared to apartment management. I kept up my walking in the evenings at the church.

The relationship between my wife and me became strained at best. Actually, it was cold during this time. She said I was "out of the will of God." I had stopped working for a member of the church and gone back to the world, back to my vomit. The way I saw it, I nearly died working for Two Mile and now had a chance to extend my life. Also, I could spend more time with my family. The new Credit Union contract lasted until June of 2007.

During those few months, I lived fully aware that my wife and those in leadership did not consider me in the will of God. I was out from under their authority. For a few months in 2005, I voluntarily went into the discipleship room hoping to appease or find some place of improvement. After a while, I locked in with someone in leadership and came out of the discipleship room in time to be in a friend's wedding at the church.

The months between June and October of 2007 were financially skinny. I looked for another Credit Union contract to replace the lost income and found none. It was odd, as tough as financial times were for the region, I expected to find work. Do you believe in destiny?

In September, to my surprise Josh Farmer contacted me. We met at a restaurant in town. He made an offer for a position with Two Mile Properties. He needed someone to take a created position easing the work load off Andy K. He called this position a regional property manager. This person would give oversight and support to the property managers at the seven apartment complexes. The position paid $40,000 a year, including a car, laptop, phone and health insurance. No surprise, the job required more than forty hours a week. There was daily travel and an occasional night in North Augusta to help the manager at the property there. Josh was professional, confident and cordial in his delivery. We had parted on good terms from my previous tour of duty, but it felt like a rock in the pit of my stomach.

Once my wife and Gerald learned about the offer, I had no peace. Almost daily, they made prodding comments until Gerald delivered a rebuke accusing me of being ungrateful and selfish. He said others in the church would jump at this opportunity. He was confused why I had not accepted the job on the spot. I delayed for two weeks. Against my internal doubts, I relented and accepted the job. My start date was October 15th.

Do you believe in providence?

My first day back at Two Mile began at 4:00AM. I drove Andy K to the airport in Columbia, SC. He was flying to China. This drive was my first time getting to know him. He was elated, almost giddy to pass off the duties pertaining to the managers. His focus turned to oversight of the ongoing apartment renovations with the hopes of cutting costs and meeting deadlines. The purpose of this two week trip to China included searching for construction materials and other items for these renovations. During his trip, I could email him, but he had limited phone access.

His parting salutation, "Submit your heart and hear Jesus. You will do fine."

And with that, I drove back to North Carolina, soon answering calls and making decisions that affected the company. Was I ready? Others thought so. Welcome to more on the job training.

Once back in the office, I met the staff. I knew them all from church, but I did not know their duties. Each one welcomed me and expressed their happiness for my return and the help I could provide. There was enough work to go around, no one should be bored.

Over the next few months, I merged into the management team, able to help in several ways. All of the managers were church members except the ones in North Augusta and Greenville. Most employees were church members. The onsite maintenance positions were filled with non-church members. Afterhours repair calls made it essential to have maintenance workers close to each complex. This mix of the two different resource groups created a few conundrums. Church members did not celebrate holidays. Non-church employees expected to not only celebrate holidays, but to be paid for the main ones. This caused a stir in some hourly, non-church employees when they realized church members were working and getting paid for holidays. Why should they be penalized for not being a church member?

During the first quarter of 2008, I started developing an employee handbook. The company was about to reach fifty employees. At that point, different laws applied and some of the inequities caused by church beliefs must be addressed. The main ones were in relation to holiday and sick pay. I found the section addressing holidays difficult to write. How to present the required verbiage and yet leave enough wiggle room for church folks to not get paid for holidays? It was a dilemma.

While in the office with Josh Farmer and two of the support staff, a small drama unfolded. The two staff workers were married to spouses who also worked for Two Mile. A comment was made about one worker from the church fielding questions from non-church employees about working on a holiday and getting paid. The non-WOFF workers were not being asked to work; however, they wanted to get paid and work. (They expected time-and-a-half or more.) One of the staff suggested a solution.

"We can give church members holiday pay and not require them to work."

Josh replied, "I don't appreciate folks from the church getting the idea they deserve a day off."

The meaning was clear. No church member could be off work and get paid for a holiday. Once I heard that comment, I mentally closed the employee handbook project, counting it as lost, never to be found again. A few days later, I made a comment to Andy K about the drama. The very next time at church, I was called into Josh's office and drilled as if I was the one in the wrong. I stood my ground and this is the only time I ever heard Josh admit to "missing it." He said he was under pressure that day, having a bad day. He did not mean the comment. The issue never was mentioned again. He did as he pleased. This ended my concern with the employee handbook.

In March, an announcement from the pulpit advised us of three days of designated prayer at the church on Monday, Tuesday, and Wednesday. The meetings started at 7:00PM sharp. Anyone not in the sanctuary and seated by then would be locked out. Their sin would be dealt with after the prayer service.

Monday evening, I barely made it in before the doors were locked. I learned later that Andy K was late. He told me he spent "time with God in his vehicle allowing his sin to be dealt with." That sounded so righteous. Tuesday, again, it was close, but I made it in the door and slid into my seat right on time. After the prayer started, Andy K made his way to my right shoulder while my wife sat at my left. During the foray of shouting and blasting; Andy leaned over starting his dissertation in my ear.

"John, you don't love your family. You stay late at work on purpose to avoid being with them."

Still louder, "I can't trust you, John. You are the King of Euphemisms."

The man who had scoffed at my life-threatening symptoms told me he could not trust me. With each accusation, I felt the pressure rising in me. These were baseless charges. This went on for two hours. During this onslaught, Gerald came over to be a part of the "prayer." He was keenly aware that I did not accept this assessment. Over and over, Andy verbally assaulted me with his venom. After a while, I withdrew inside myself, just hoping for the meeting to come to an end.

Finally, as the meeting came to a close, I stood up telling Andy, "I have to go to the restroom."

"You are a liar," he said.

At that moment, I came close to flattening his Irish nose, but, I let him breathe another few minutes while I pushed passed his arrogant self, making a bee-line to the restroom. Thankfully, he did not touch me or try to stop me. These emotions return as I write this account six years later. In the restroom, I found the strength to pass on the physical altercation which I knew would cost me more than he was worth. The service ended with no additional volleys from Andy. Later that evening, I calmed down enough to go walking around the church.

The next morning at the office, Andy appeared all cheery. I sat across from him while he worked on an advertising project for renovated apartments. The owners decided to put used recycled appliances in "newly renovated" apartments.

He spoke out, "I am having a hard time coming up with the right words for these advertisements."

Where others could hear, he chirped, "John, you are good with words, come over here and help me with this."

I looked at him showing no emotion. "No."

I hoped he would stay on his side of the office. The patronizing gall of making that comment and expecting me to come help him was too much. If the comments the night before had not been enough, that morning I lost any and all respect for the man. He was a shining, prime example of someone I never wanted to become. By some unknown grace, I managed to survive the next couple weeks. The excitement for this job had disappeared and I knew it.

March passed with no further incidents.

CHAPTER TWENTY-FIVE

APRIL 9, 2008 WAS A WEDNESDAY

When running late for a service at WOFF, eating is not a priority. Just get in and take your seat, stay awake, appear interested, take hold and know you are being watched. The end of this evening service brought another meeting for me.

A voice from the podium, "John Huddle, meet in Ray's office."

My thoughts raced. What had I done? Immediately, I reviewed the last few hours: where, who, what, when, why? Though these meetings were not unusual, after the internal checklist, no alarms went off in my thinking. Many a night was spent in Ray's office after a church service planning, reviewing and managing the next crisis for my employer, Two Mile Properties.

The first awareness of a strange breeze blowing occurred when I saw my wife standing outside the office door in the fellowship hall. She was as nervous as a bridled filly waiting to jump and run. Her nervousness should have sounded a loud alarm, but I missed it.

I asked, "Why are you here? Where are the children?"

"The children are taken hold of," she answered avoiding my gaze at every point.

Martha's name had not been called. Wading through the hallway hustle and bustle, that narrow artery teaming with children and adults moving along their chosen path, my thoughts caught a glimpse of the hidden truth--she knew the purpose of the meeting. Her expression portrayed angst and yet, I was unsure.

"Will you be in this meeting?"

Her nod sent uneasiness into the pit of my stomach.

This was not a business meeting. Sirens wailed. Thoughts bombarded my mind, waves of fear washed over me leaving their residue. Why did the owners call my wife into this meeting?

Even then, it was hard to accept one of the "living mantras" of WOFF: Each part of your life is subject to "the will of God." In order to know and live in "the will of God," every part of your life is interconnected and subject to the ever-changing, more intrusive and far-reaching control dynamics of WOFF as administered by the leader, Jane Whaley. She heard God for everyone, reaching into every part of your life. "Sin in your life" kept you from knowing God's will.

The next few hours changed my life in ways only known by Providence.

Time seemed suspended while I stood outside the office door. As a leader in the church, Ray had an office that served many purposes. Soon, he approached in his slow and deliberate fashion. He sported a look which was meant to put me at ease. I recognized his gentle nature when he brought truth to someone. We exchanged greetings as he unlocked the door and motioned for us to come inside. I took a seat in a small corner at the front of the desk. My wife stood at my left side as he made motions for more folks to crowd into the room. Josh took the seat behind the desk. As an attorney and owner of Two Mile, his words carried weight. During the short awkward exchanges of those filing in, it quickly became evident that everyone else had been briefed about the proceedings.

Those in attendance included former pastors of the Greenville church, Gerald Southerland, and his wife, Linda. Also present, Andy K. He entered the room looking assured of his purpose. Andy, an intelligent and deliberate fellow, never ignored the levels of authority inside WOFF, however at times, showed flashes of self desire betraying his shiny coat.

About 9:30PM, Ray led off with a why we are all here statement, "Josh brought some things to my attention that pertain to you…"

Josh took the lead in a much stronger fashion. "If I had known what was going on earlier, I would have addressed this sooner. Andy tells me that you have been spending too many hours on your part-time Credit Union work; your focus has been more on that than with Two Mile."

This statement made me think this was an extension of the impromptu meeting during the recent prayer session in March, when Andy confronted me. Wrongly, I assumed the fallout from that meeting had been averted.

All in attendance remained solemn waiting for Josh to finish and for me to react to his assessment. His ending ultimatum included, "…tonight, you will quit your part-time job or you will be fired from Two Mile Properties."

Life inside WOFF required synergy. My part-time Credit Union work remained a sticking point for years in the group's quest to own me. This position left me "out from under authority."

An awkward silence settled over us as I considered an acceptable and accurate reply. "I have a real problem with that."

This initial refusal to accept Josh's assessment as the will of God brought the next level of reviews of my worth as a person. Andy pointed out a time when I left the job to pay a bill.

Yes, I did but felt justified with all the hours I put in to take some time for personal business. That answer did not stop their fury; it sent the personal rebukes to a new level.

Then, Brooke C. blew into the room. Her position of leadership set her at a level of authority surpassing all others in the room. The length of this meeting instantly extended to indefinite. Brooke announced, "There must be the unclean in your life since you could not immediately accept and embrace 'the will of God' for the job change."

The scope and pace of the accusations increased at this point, moving from job-related infractions to my intimate relationship and private time with my wife. We were registering at least an EF-3 on the tornado scale. Their demands increased in an attempt to elicit a confession of whatever sin obviously resided in my heart.

"What is it, John? What is the sin so deep which you have hidden for years that is taking you over?

"That sin is blinding you to God's will, right now! Tell us, let us blast it and get you help…"

"Whatever it is, it is holding you back from taking your place …."

"We love you, you know that. We want to help you…"

Brooke summed up the barrage, "If you were right with God, you would be able to accept the will of God, immediately, no matter what!"

The session continued. Brooke and the others took turns berating and pounding me in an effort to open my heart and make me confess my sin. Once a new accusation was pronounced, everyone stared and waited for me to confess to something.

During these silent stare sessions, I drifted into a dream-like state. The people chattered around me, but my understanding slowed. Any response I did give had to be forced from my mouth. I knew the wrongness surrounding this whole scene, yet I felt powerless to change or stop it. With all that was in me I wanted to forget this night all together and get up and run.

While in this dream-like state, I realized each person in the room believed the way I was treated was normal and acceptable. That realization soon became the seed of strength which grew and caused me to leave WOFF.

After about ninety minutes, I did what I later learned other survivors did. I agreed and confessed something in hopes to end the onslaught. In hindsight, I know the subject of my confession didn't matter. Obtaining a confession cemented me deeper under their control.

After this useless admission, Jane Whaley stormed in the room, poked her finger in my obviously confused face and screamed, "You are full of the unclean!"

At that point, in unison, those around me blurted out, "You cut your eyes at her! That was a devil!"

Suddenly, memories of other members telling of moments like this flooded my mind. They talked of meeting the "authority of God." Up until then, I had no idea what they were saying. Never had my inner personal space been invaded as much as in this meeting. The sea of activity spun out of control as I clung to my racing thoughts seeking shelter and finding none.

Next, Jane turned on my crying wife, "And you let him be this way!"

Jane left the room muttering she had other meetings.

My wife, catching the spirit of the EF-5 blowing through the room began screaming at me, "Repent and start crying out to God!"

At that exhortation, my hopes to end this trauma session rested on leaning over and doing my best to at least feign some behaviors accepted by WOFF as repentance. I knew it to be shallow at best, since the dream-like session left me past feeling, as if under a dose of anesthesia. I retreated into the inner part of my being while watching this horror movie unfold around me. Even my hearing lessened and some rebukes had to be repeated.

After two and a half hours, I still refused to give in to the screaming, rebukes and WOFF-reasoning. Brooke reached for the phone, calling for Jane's direction, "Jane, we are not getting anywhere here, I think we need to quit."

Once she uttered, "Okay," and hung-up, the meeting broke up. So odd; no one else seemed affected in the least by the winds of destruction that had blown me over.

My wife asked Josh, "Does he go to work on Thursday?"

By this time, Josh was in the hallway. "I don't need anyone like that working for me."

And with that, I was fired. I surrendered the company car and the laptop.

The rolling drama did not end when I left the church grounds. After a solemn ride home with my wife, the children already in bed, my wife exclaimed, "You don't sleep in this bed!"

Shell shocked, I slept in the recliner. Honestly, who wanted to be next to her at that time?

I remember waking up the next morning to an empty feeling. Was it all a dream? Would things go back to normal and mend themselves? No. The destruction set on course by the tornado force winds that blew into my life was real. The damage was only beginning to be felt.

I lived through Hurricane Hugo in 1989 and experienced the aftermath. Thursday was the morning after the storm. The damage assessment began. I spent the day wandering, wondering and thinking, *What if things were different? Can we fix this? What do I do from here?* Though I could not see into the future, my world had forever changed.

By the next night, I gathered my courage telling my wife "I am sleeping in my bed. If you don't like it, you can sleep in the recliner." We slept in the bed on our separate edges, not touching. No doubt, after that evening, our relationship was on a downhill slide.

April 9th marked our 20th wedding anniversary. In WOFF, this was not a reason to celebrate. Instead of joy, we were headed on a path which included previously unknown intense emotions. We could not predict the impact of the events unfolding over the coming months and years,. Now, the overwhelming irony of this meeting and the destruction it unleashed is hard to believe

CHAPTER TWENTY-SIX

AFTER THE STORM

The initial few days after being fired were a blur. I was told to come to the morning prayer meeting. I don't remember if I did. I learned later that Josh asked my wife if I planned to ask for my job back. What an insult. All I could think was no, I never planned on asking for that job back.

After getting my last paycheck, I could see things were going to be tight soon unless something changed. Before I started my second tour at Two Mile, I found a part-time contract at a Credit Union about an hour from the house. That one contract had not been enough to keep us going, and thus I agreed to take the full time job.

I called that Credit Union, and they renewed my contract with an increase. I was excited, but my wife did not share my feelings. For me, it was an answer to prayer. I could provide for my family and not have to be gone fifty to sixty hours a week. I returned to that Credit Union before the end of April. My two contracts and the salary Martha received from the school were enough to keep us going.

My status inside the church again was unsure as in the years of 2005 to 2007; I had refused to bend to the pressures of the top leader and her second in command. I was "out from under authority" but had replaced the lost income. I did not agree with the way leadership treated me. In addition, Brooke started her marriage classes up again and pressures to control our private lives increased. All of this, added to my daughter's pending June 1st graduation, made for an unstable time.

The second Tuesday in May, I drove to Marion for work. Somewhere near the small town of Gilkey, I passed over a dead skunk in the road. Suddenly, I remembered a song. "Dead Skunk in the Middle of the Road." I sang the chorus and all the words I knew.

Oh, what rebellion. No faithful member sang that song. But, I sang it over and over and louder each time. Something changed on the inside. When I arrived at the Credit Union, I played the song for a few other employees. They laughed; I laughed. After wearing that one out, I found Kate Smith singing "God Bless America." I played that one so loud the manager came by and told me to turn it down. Oh, the more it played the more excited I got. Yes, God Bless America! We can live free in America!

During those days, I had two thoughts that gave me such hope and yet at the same time were weighty. First, WOFF was subject to being called a cult because the members feared Jane Whaley more than God.

The second thought was the term "shepherding movement." Years earlier, I had heard of this movement but knew I needed to research it. Once I did, I knew why. The error of the leadership in that movement was being repeated before my eyes. I could not tell anyone inside the group. If Jane learned my thoughts, I would be barred from my daughter's graduation which I desperately wanted to attend. I kept these thoughts to myself and sang about dead skunks and God Bless America, day after day. The weeks in May passed slowly. I worked and returned home doing the best I could to feign my submission to the church practices. However, inside me grew the realization that we were being duped.

As customary, high school seniors submitted their list of invitations to the office for approval. The invitation list for my daughter included my mom, stepfather, my sister, her husband and son. This was their first visit to the church. All exciting and yet there was an underlying apprehension.

This May was the year that Jane revealed the senior girls were "homely." The resulting changes were sudden and effective. Homely had no place in that class any more. All of this newness added to the expectations surrounding the whole event.

The graduation practices proceeded and the testimonies reviewed and rehearsed. The dresses and make-up choices were approved. The list for food was finalized, the worker lists were set. There were previous graduations, but this one was special to our family because our daughter was graduating.

The day finally arrived. The relatives arrived as promised. Pushing through any awkwardness, we greeted them and the reception was warm. My family arrived in time as did Martha's. We escorted them to their seats.

The graduation show went off without a hitch. Jane made her speech, diplomas were handed out, pictures were taken at the allotted times and the reception line formed as normal. The whole night was full of hugs and smiles. This occasion was one of the few times gifts were given between members. The anticipation over these gifts increased the excitement.

I accompanied my family through the reception area. As we passed through the hall, Jane made the effort to speak to me and my mom. The exchange included Jane bragging about her grandson. She proclaimed his class was taking "standardized testing," and they were scoring much higher than grade level. She also explained his resistance to the "math devil." My mom chuckled and later retold the whole conversation in detail. When time for my family to leave, I escorted them to their cars and thanked them for coming. There were hugs and more smiles. They were staying in a local hotel and left the next day without further contact.

After their departure, I went inside to take pictures of my daughter, her class, and of her gifts. The pictures were full of smiles. For seniors, graduating and receiving a diploma was considered an accomplishment. It was a grand evening. Underneath my joy as I took the pictures was an ever-increasing, gnawing feeling that things could change after this event. I had no idea the swiftness and severity of those changes.

CHAPTER TWENTY-SEVEN

YOU ARE OUT OF
THE CHURCH

The excitement of graduation passed, the tensions in our home remained. Inside, I knew we were heading for unchartered waters. What I did not anticipate was the slow train wreck coming to leave me reeling with bewilderment.

A few days after graduation, I called Lora B. She and her husband had "helped" my wife and me for a few months. Even before we all moved from Greenville, Lora positioned herself as a short link to Jane. She loved to pray loud, having the raspy voice as evidence.

Once our conversation started, I knew this was the time to take the dive. I outlined the two thoughts which I first had several weeks earlier. In response to the first statement, WOFF was subject to being called a cult because the members feared Jane more than God, Lora initially agreed, then backstroked.

The reason for her backtracking may have been that English was not her native language. She was Finnish. Some of the nuances of certain phrases were difficult for her to catch. I knew she would not knowingly go on record against Jane. She tried to dissuade me of the accuracy of the statement.

Her arguments included: "Look at the children. You know so many folks see how our children are so respectful and well-behaved. Do you deny that? Can this not be of God?"

My reactions did not confirm her reasoning; she knew her efforts were not working.

I shared the second phrase, Shepherding movement. She admitted she was not aware of the movement. I took time to briefly explain it. She denied the similarities. Soon, she excused herself saying she would call me back.

About three hours later, her number appeared on my phone. I answered, and she started a calm explanation of what had happened in the previous conversation. She had reached Jane and relayed our conversation.

Lora said, "I told her what you said. She said you were out of the church."

"Excuse me?"

"She said you are being put out of the church. You need to cry out to God."

Inside, I had expected some form of discipline. In WOFF-speak, this was a heavy statement. In times past, I had been "in discipleship" which meant separated from normal activities but still in the church. Members in discipleship were segregated during services and may be prohibited from other activities which were not essential to "hearing the word." Being "out of the church" was a new place for me.

Immediately, I realized this could bring many changes. If I had known the full range of changes at that moment, my reaction may have been different.

Later that evening I went to the church and walked around the parking lot. The next day, Lora called me again.

"Word has gotten back to Jane that you were at the church walking. She wants it clear, you are not allowed on church property, for any reason."

I may have replied, I don't recall. There was anger over such an edict and in my thinking my walking was not to interact with others but to continue my exercise routine. My times walking around the church were over. I knew that the church grounds were private property, and Jane could police them as she wished. I accepted the new barrier.

Within the next few days, I called my mom to talk to her about the graduation. There were other things we could talk about, but I knew we needed to start with the week before.

I asked, "What did you think of the graduation?"

She hesitated. I knew she knew of the possible repercussions for saying anything against the church.

"Why do you ask?"

"I am having some trouble with some things in the church."

"It was rehearsed like a production or show."

I laughed, "Well, yeah, you are right."

"It was so obvious; each graduate used the same Scriptures and cried almost at the exact same place as the rest of them. What is going on?"

"I am having trouble with some things."

"I will help you any way I can."

What a relief. I had no idea at the time, but, with that offer, I started a slow exit from WOFF. Knowing there was help available allowed the idea to stand at the edge of my consciousness until I was ready to consider leaving as a viable choice.

What other things the conversation included, I don't remember. I may have mentioned being put out of the church. I promised to call her again in a few days, making certain I had her email address.

It took several more weeks to even accept the idea of leaving WOFF and my family. The idea of a permanent divide never was considered during my initial stages of planning or the first few months after I left.

I waivered with many doubts over the choice to leave. I experienced an agony that went deep and brought with it mountains of uncertainty. Leaving was not as easy as packing the van and backing out of the driveway. It is hard to say exactly when I accepted the idea of leaving. In the narrative supported by emails in the next chapter, I first mention having made my decision to leave on June 22nd. I remember thinking, as the planning started and the day was set, is this happening? Am I leaving my family and those who I have considered my friends up until this whole mess imploded? Am I leaving them? How did we get here?

It is ludicrous to think I have to write, "I loved my family." But, I loved my family and that realization was even more difficult to process as I grew severely distraught at the shunning I experienced once I was put out of the church. My own family as well as the other family in the house faithfully shunned me.

This meant the other family refused to speak to me or acknowledge my presence. They ignored me even when in the same room. My children said very few words to me, becoming colder to my attempts at conversation. After I was put out of the church in the first week of June, I ate only a few meals with my children until I left in July. If my wife decided to eat in my presence, the meal was overrun by silence or with her constant berating and probing me to "repent and get right with God." Getting right with God only occurred by talking to Jane. The interactions between my family and I dwindled to zero.

As the days passed, the great lengths my wife went to in order to keep my children from me surprised, angered and shocked me. At first, she played coy and nonchalant. She left me voice mails stating that we were eating separately. The children were with their friends. I saved the voice mails for months until I was forced to get a new phone. When doubt came over my move away from the group, I played the voicemails full of her excuses for not eating with me or allowing the children to spend time with me. These voice mails proved enough to reinforce my decision to leave the emotionally caustic setting.

The accompanying angst over this shunning behavior filled my thinking. It exploded in my conversations and my emails to my mom. She reacted with disbelief and shock, warning and encouraging me to take care of myself..

I stayed longer hours at the Credit Union. Why rush to get back to the deafening silence and the frozen reception? During weekends, I spent time at the Credit Union even when there was no work to complete. Sometimes, I did research on the computer and sent emails.

One night, as I meandered back into the house hoping to find everyone asleep, I entered the bedroom to find Martha awake. She had been crying.

She blurted out, "Are you cheating on me?"

This question shook me to the seriousness of the whole charade. The thought of her asking such a question cut me deeply. I told her I stayed at the Credit Union where there were security cameras filming me. "There is not anything else going on."

She did not act like she believed me and why should she?. For her to even think there was another female drawing me away from our family collapse indicated how out of focus things were. This slow train wreck we were living through tossed and turned us like fodder in the wind. We were all reacting and grieving the death of our family over my decision to leave this subculture. The requirement "repent and cry out to God" meant admitting that WOFF life was the life for me. Return and again embrace the daily controls. That was not going to happen, I had learned too much. The requirements on my family to do whatever it took to bring me back into "the will of God" were taxing and overwhelming for them.

CHAPTER TWENTY-EIGHT

THE SLOW TRAIN WRECK

The following narrative is a compilation from emails to my mom and brother during June and July of 2008. They are edited and formatted for this purpose. My hope is for this narrative to give some indication of the depth and intensity of the emotional struggles during this time. Of course, even in this effort, I acknowledge this will be only my admissions to others. My internal struggles went beyond words, written or spoken.

While writing this account, I searched emails from the time period of June and July 2008. During that period, I stayed in daily contact with my mom and later, my brother. Reading these emails and reflecting on the emotional content ignited the memories bringing back much of the sickening turmoil of those days. I relived the scenes which included the highly emotional conversations, the body postures, the facial expressions and the hurt. I again heard the words that brought the division causing my family to implode. I stopped writing this manuscript for six weeks as I processed and sought stability before starting again.

After six weeks of searching, talking to others and acquiring a new resolve, I restarted the process of telling this story. The point of return to the task of sharing this tragedy came with the following thoughts:

First, this story must be told in order to pull back the thick curtains holding the secrets of the destructive dynamics inside of WOFF.

Second, I am persuaded and want to make clear that by telling this story, I do not blame my wife and children for how they responded or acted during this drama. We were marionettes on strings. This drama was being overseen and played by the head Puppet Master. During the previous years, we were conditioned to play the parts we acted out. With each sermon, each public display of correction, each small group or class attended the dye was set

All of these measures end in the conditions for us which were stated in the Findings of Facts in the McGee Custody case. (Rutherford County District Court File no.-00-CVD 0686) Like the McGees, my wife and I lost control of our family. This happened as each parent was required to "lock-in with leadership before decisions were made in the family." The stark reality was that we were not a family in any normal sense of the meaning, but a group of four individuals living out a life in the same house. We loved each other, that I am sure. But, the relational dynamics were subverted by the daily controls exerted over us. All of these were presented as "God's will." There was love between us, but no matter the depth of the love, the dynamics for displaying that love rested on the foundation of Jane and whatever Jane said was the will of God. The conditioning of the past and the directions during the drama led us down a path that many families and individuals from this group had previously traveled.

My wife called for immediate input from church leaders after an encounter with me. For proof of this, I checked her cell phone records for a few weeks after this crisis began. After a discussion or conflict between my wife and me, almost every time, my wife called the Southerlands. I knew they were not talking about the weather. She reported, and then received the next strategy to combat what I said or did. This was a result of the training inside the group.

The drive to tell this story does not include any desire to hold the players in this drama to their past. Telling the secrets of this past does not limit their future, as living through it did not dictate or limit mine. My, now, ex-wife and my children can each have a change of mind and heart and, if they choose, leave WOFF. Members can and do find ways to break the strings of the Puppet Master. By telling this story, I encourage others to cut the strings and find their own way in life. For the leader and the leadership, my hope is not as strong that they will change; but none of them should be limited by my hope.

Early in the unfolding of these events, I became keenly aware of my choices upon my children. Yet, looking back, I knew they were experiencing internal struggles which were beyond words and outside of the accepted conversation structure for group members.

By June 8th, one week after my daughter's graduation, I started sharing my struggles with emails to my mom. Since I was not allowed to attend the church services, the opportunity to communicate was plentiful. The following is one of the first emails to my mom, shortly after her initial offer to help:

Sun, 8 Jun 2008 2:10 pm
Mom,

Consider the children's world. When Daddy starts backing up and apparently rejecting what has been taught for all their known lives, how easy is it to correlate that to rejecting them, personally. It is a serious matter, and I need wisdom how to walk with them.
Prayers requested,
John
*****

Early in the shunning episodes, I considered my options for taking cover and seeking a place of refuge away from the barrage of silence. In an email explaining my conversation with my father-in-law, I reveal the painful options being considered.

Sun, 8 Jun 2008 11:13 am
Mom,

I called [father-in-law] and he was not surprised. He said they would be praying and asked me not to do anything rash. Suppose I am a sluggard for a while. I can't see how this will work for very long. I am anticipating a big confrontation with powers that be- "submit or leave and take the load for destroying your family." I have considered getting a place near my office in Marion. Oh, I can't go that direction in my thoughts for very long. It is painful. More as I know.
John
*****

Even though I was not allowed to attend services, I was still considered under the requirements to be contrite and "humbly seeking a place of repentance." I explain the process below.

Jun 8, 2008
Mom,

Well, the house is quiet, except for the computer and the fans... There are many dynamics involved here. Either during or after this evening's services, I will be asked the question, "Well, what are you hearing? Are you ready to call Gerald yet and get help?" Someone will either call my cell phone or Martha will ask me tonight- under direct approval of course of "leadership." Gerald is the under pastor that I have not talked to in weeks since he chewed on me real bad about taking the Credit Union work again...(April) There is also the dynamic of not knowing what was said this morning and no one volunteering to telling and me not daring to ask... (that was not right to ask. I am out of the church...) So, I am supposed to care and that is to drive me to come to some place of contrition and come up with some statement that will lead me to call Gerald and make some sort of expression of needing help, prayer or something. I am supposed to come to some acknowledgment of how evil I have been to not go directly and ask questions and how evil it was to go out on the Internet to seek answers and some sort of other thing about how I know "God" would not have it that way and ......? Do you see the picture?

And the longer I wait the more wicked I am and the longer I wait, the more gross my sin and the more probable it is that I would have to "talk" to Jane W. in person to even come back into the church and into the sanctuary. It is no doubt, talking to Gerald will just be a step for a "meeting with Jane"....

There has arisen the question as yet unanswered; will I be allowed to continue walking at the church in the evenings like I have been? Tonight, I am supposed to get that answer. If that is a "no"- then it is real serious. I have never "crossed" that line before... so to speak. If that answer is "no" my time here may be shorter than I think...
(concerning the next day...)

I will go to work and be pretty much unaffected—except subject to a phone call any minute that could change my living arrangements or anything else....? Isn't this whole deal surreal? It is hard to believe I have lived like this for so long. (accepting this as normal) I once told someone here that I had problems with one person having so much control over my life-- Jane's decisions about this whole deal affect me - drastically. I was told it is not her decisions- she was giving us God's word and decision...(?) or (!) BOTH
More as I know...
John
*****

As I later learned, I was involved in "playing the game" as many do before they leave WOFF. Timing of an exit from such a group is critical, at least in the minds of those involved. In my case, the shunning drama would move my time table to be shorter than I ever imagined. Another email from the same day.

Jun 8, 2008

Mom,

In some respects, until I know the right course I will have to "play the game" or I may be forced out too early. I played it for 3 long weeks before graduation. Now, we are in the second half - so to speak. There is a favorite phrase used around here from the top on down... "When someone is deceived- they're deceived." Ironic to say the least. If my family was not deceived they would not treat me this way. I hope to be able to show them God's love and never once let them think that I don't love them, though the separation is obvious.... The children are really feeling it.

*****

The message I was given came in several parts with one goal: humble myself and go back under Jane's control. Of course, it was not said in those words. And to that extent, my inner struggles to know the difference between what is reality and what it is not became intense. The stark truth remains that faithful members say they serve God and walk with God's people while their service to God is solely dependent on their submission to Jane. There is the outward speech which belies the inward knowing. Thus the stress and struggles are renamed submitting to God's will.

June 9, 2008

Mom,

I have been told "Everyone goes through the same door of humility". (Translate: everyone has been humiliated by leadership and those who stayed accepted it and liked it and wanted more of it...?? It is good for you...)

I have been told: "You are so full of pride - humble yourself and cry out to God so he can change your wicked heart." (Translate: you don't conform to what has been preached and accepted by everyone else and that makes for a hard time for some of us. If you don't walk the line, it can lead others away from believing this stuff. Others may go to hell because you don't submit, we can't have that....)

I have been told: "Your children are watching you... you need to set the example." (Translate: the children do watch, and if I don't conform, "we" will tell them you are full of rebellion and going to hell... don't copy him, don't follow him... don't open your heart to him...)

I have been told: "How can you doubt what God is doing here? Look at the children and how well they are doing and how well they 'take hold'." (Translate: our children are what we depend on to stem the tide of accusations of any kind of wrong doing... Since they look and behave so well, we must be doing fine or better than anyone else. Our children do so well academically; it has to be the approval of God on us.)

back to work... maybe...
*****

Everything is subject to the unwritten rules of the group, even the background pictures on your computer.
Sat, 14 Jun 2008 1:21 pm
Mom,

I feel like some things may come to a head tomorrow. Since, I don't plan to submit to the stay at home thing. There could be a confrontation. But, I am almost past feeling in the whole situation.
Last night, I showed Martha where I had put a picture of Michael and Sarah from graduation night on the desktop background. She looked and at first said it was nice. Then she froze for a slight second. Later, I remembered one of the "rules"- don't put people's pictures on desktop backgrounds for computers that will be out in the world. I had broken a rule. She did not say anything, yet. But, this computer always stays with me. So we shall see. I like the picture and it stays- until I find a better one…
John

This is an outtake of an email to a dear friend, who I have known for over 20 years:

June 20, 2008
"...My wife and children count me as reprobate and will not even return an "I love you, too" when saying good night!!!!!!!!!!!!! It is like a walking nightmare...
...I have been staying away from home because the reception is arctic. The meals together are stiff and only with Martha repeating the mantra of the church...."
*****

By June 22nd, I am revealing my plan to leave and the reason why.

Jun 22, 2008
Mom,
In a nutshell, the reason I think I need to leave at least for the afternoon is that it is hard to be around ones that are supposed to talk (and) to love you and they won't talk to you. Understand?
John
*****

From June 8th when I mentioned the pain of the thought of leaving until June 22[nd,] you can you see how crushing the effect of the shunning had become. While my whole world crumbled around me, I searched for a place of safety. Contrary to what those around me believed, this was not at the feet of the group leader. Two days later, the reactions of my children were a concern.

Sent: Tue, 24 Jun 2008 9:37 am

What is being done to me is not illegal in man's eyes. But, I believe God sees it another way. Sarah walked out of the kitchen when I walked in and nary spoke a word and Michael is still hard. They are being led and coached I say first by their mother. Then, it is being reinforced by the "leadership"   Many are they [who] rise up against me, many are they that [think] of my soul- there is no hope for him in God, But thou oh Lord art a shield for me the glory and the lifter of my head!!!

*****

Jun 24, 2008

Mom,

The children are being told, "How can you honor or fellowship with someone who has turned their back on God and that which God has given them?" It is almost a "whatever it takes to bring him back to humility in God" attitude. That is no exaggeration. So, when they see me dismayed at the 'no touch, no talk' restraint, they think they are winning. That is one reason I need to stay away during the day as much as possible. More as I know.

Love,

John

*****

June 27, 2008 - Friday

Mom,

I am not sure of all I will be doing [the next day]. Martha only has plans to stay around, clean house and get "ready for seminar." So, if I try to talk to her and it does not go well, I will be "going to work." Actually, I am planning on working, need the beans. So, it could be good or it could be another rotten Saturday. Pretty sure none of us will be up too early. From there the schedule is not set. But, with tonight's reaffirmation of WOFF values and such, I could get the "mantra." If that is the case, I either fight it with what I know to be truth or leave... (Or both...)

Love you...

John

During this time, I purchased the book, *Churches That Abuse*, By Ronald Enroth. It seems like a contradictory title, but if you are used to abuse, similar to the way I grew used to the pains in my chest before the heart attack, you need someone to point out the abuses. This book was a great help. I recommend it. It opened my eyes to some of the unsafe practices of WOFF.

Jun 27, 2008
To Mom

Well, I was able to help Martha with some peanut butter balls. Just to spend time with her. No real conversation, except she asked, "Where are you? Translate- have you heard where your sin is and can you repent? I told her I had questions and was just trying not to lose relationship with Jesus.

She asked, "Have you called to get help?"
Translate- did you call anyone from the church?

"No."

"You better." Translate- I am worried you won't be allowed back in. (I don't care) She just does not get it. Saturday may be a day we can talk...I realize our relationship has been based on church activities. Take that out and we are "lost." So sad. We need to re-group and remember we married each other, not a church.

Love you,

John

*****

On July 1st, I had an explosive exchange with my daughter. She mentioned something about me coming back to God.

I said, "Coming back to God may not include going back to WOFF."

She exclaimed, "I will not go to hell with you. I am staying in the move of God!"

I left the house and drove to McDonalds to calm down. Later, Martha called to ask where I was. She said, "You can come home, now."

Again, we slept on our edges of the bed, if we slept at all.

Jul 2, 2008
Mom,

Here is the latest- in brief. I got home about 1AM.

Martha said, "Do you have anything to say?"

I told her I am certain Sarah told her what I said. From there Martha volunteered to "listen," but not really. I think she just wanted to tell me how wrong I was. I began to tell her the thoughts I was having that lead me to wanting to know more about [the] "shepherding movement" and other things. I told [her] some about the book, *Churches that Abuse*.

That is when she sat up and said, "You need major help."

I tried to point out to her how many areas of our life are controlled and if a certain person doesn't "feel good" about a decision we were not supposed to do it.

I said, "That is not God's way."

She chuckled and said, "All the leaders were trying to do was [us] help hear God."

(I should have quit here because she is so duped that no one here has any ulterior motives - like taking Miracle offerings every week!)
She may say she wants to listen, but she just wanted enough to twist and tell me how wrong I was... if people are not ready to hear, then I should not have wasted my breathe or my night.
(In reference to losing the job with Two Mile Properties) She said "You didn't get fired."

Wow. Then I realized she was not at the end of the hallway when the owner said it. So, she has believed all this time, I walked away. Truth is when I was given the ultimatum to quit the part time work, I said, "I have a hard time with that," and the meeting ended. (4/9) I was told to "stay home until you get your heart right" (Translate- stay away until you see I'm right (the owner) and then we will see if you can come back to work.)

There is more to tell, but at the end I turned it on her and told her that regardless if she and the children ever see any of what I said, I will go on and serve God, seek God with or without them. She was taken back for a minute. That was her line. I told her everything I ever believed about God and going to church is being shaken and re-considered. I told her my search doesn't assume the ending place is WOFF.

She said that since, "God told us to come in 2002, then this is where we need to be."

I told her, "I know a lot more now than in 2002 about what "being here" means. I am not sure about staying." She then wanted to pray, (translate – "preach pray" where someone pretends they are talking to God to tell you how you should be and what you should pray and how you should be thinking- MAJOR control tool that makes me SICK! I have done it on occasion, but now- No!) It is so repulsive! And false!!!! I took about as much as I could take and stopped her and patted my pillow and told her I wanted to sleep.

Net: she is oblivious and not ready to hear. This whole deal is totally my fault and no one else EVER did or does anything wrong. When I told her that the way I was treated Saturday was not God, she only gave the slight blink and nod motion.

She said, "We are all just crying out for your life that you will turn back to God and come out from this "witchcraft." (Translate- repent and come back to WOFF.)

I told her that the way I was treated (shunned) was NOT drawing me closer to God, her, the family or anyone else. Nothing she or the children were doing was causing me to hunger for God or repent for anything. I told her I had sin God wanted to deal with as does everyone.

At that point she says the mantra, "Then come get help and expose it and get 'prayer.'"

I told her during the conversation that the mantras made me sick. I had to explain what a mantra was...

Love,

John

P.S. Tired- rushed out of house as soon as I could. She "exhorted" me to get in my Bible and cry out for answers. I can, but so far she does not want to hear the Scriptures I am hearing.

Before I forget, Sarah started out last night then launched into the – *"You should be grateful you are still alive, Dad! God could strike you dead with the rebellion you are giving to."*

That is when I knew she needed a small statement about what I think about the WOFF.

*****

I consider the events above as the turning points which lead me to finalize my plans to leave. Up until that night, I may have been persuaded to stay, though in a suspended state. I don't blame my daughter for anything. She repeated what she had been conditioned to say and to feel. When my wife rejected my explanations and said I needed "major help," I signed the lease for an apartment. I saw only future shunning and rejection from everyone in my family whom I dearly loved. Too much to take. I no longer believed with any part of my being that salvation only came through membership at WOFF. I was no longer able to pretend. The attempts to get me to lock-in intensified.

Sent: Tue, 1 Jul 2008 11:13 am

Mom,

This morning I endured a very slanted impassioned plea from Martha to call someone from WOFF and get help. She began by reciting two conversations we had in our dating years. She says I espoused a desire to be a minister. I am sure I did. (But, my idea of who or what that was/is- was so twisted at that time- as we discussed in subsequent conversations since that time.) Anyway, I say I endured because toward the end she rebuked me for the look on my face. My thoughts were such that I wanted to respond, but for some reason couldn't in full measure.

I went out the door saying- "I have a lot to say"-- knowing she may not be ready to hear.

I know it sounds weird, but if she does not listen to the next big attempt for me to talk to her, then I need a place to live. Knowing that has kept me back from trying again. Of course, I rehearsed the conversation on the way to Marion... WRONG. That is not what I need to do...

After reading what little I have in this new book, I see that the one fact alone of being more afraid of the WOFF leader than God should suffice for myself or anyone else to leave. That one fact and/or observation should alert anyone that things in their heart (my heart) are not right, regardless of the surroundings and how it all happened. All subsequent observations should pale to the understanding that anyone should take the place of God in my heart or anyone else's. (1John 5:21) In light of that, all other observations still may need to be considered at some point. That one "truth" of fearing a person more than God is foundational for all else at WOFF to continue. I was aware of that before my last round of being put out of the church.

Next, I looked up information on "Shepherding Movement." That second notion was affirming the first, unbeknownst to me at the start. Once word got back to Jane that I had done that- I was put out. And the absolute denial of being involved in anything like that was told to me from her through others. (if it waddles and quacks like a duck...)

I am going through a time of examining everything I thought I knew was true and just seeing what settles out. What have I believed and what have I done in agreement with those beliefs and how have I ordered my life around those beliefs? It is shaking me to deep levels and I see Martha considering things she may not have recently. However, until we have some time to talk freely, I will not know what direction she is headed. Right now, I fear she is "toeing the party line" so to speak.

In a little while I need to be on the road. I can call...

Love,

John

*****

Sarah also said "...you either serve God (being at WOFF was the meaning) or you serve the devil. If you won't follow God- (WOFF), you serve the devil..."

To my brother on July 6th:

It looks like this coming week I will be able to move to the 2 bedroom apartment. Details are still to be worked out and I have not told Martha and the children. I believe Martha still harbors false hopes of my return to Word of (slavery) Faith. But, it is not going to happen.

I told Mom on the one hand I know this is the next step, but on the other, I am scared, too. It seems so drastic. But, so has been the change toward me from my own family. It has been an emotional upheaval to put it mildly. To them Daddy, as he once was, does not exist. Daddy is not "in the church-serving God."

Martha and I had an exchange on Saturday. Where I told her I was going to Marion before she got home.

She says, "So, you are not tired of your stubbornness?"

I told her I was not welcome here.

She said "Because of what you are giving to."

I told her I would not try to convince her anymore, it was not my purpose.

Her reply, "It is dangerous what you are doing."

I said, "It is dangerous to stay." (Meaning in the house)

She changed subjects and retreated into her deceptive "bliss." She has to have a knowing that I am making plans. Who in their right mind would sign up for an endless supply of this "shunning" stuff? To be around those that are supposed to love you and they won't talk to you except to tell you are deceived and going to HELL! is quite difficult to say the least. Where is the true love of God in any of this? "Slave Faith" is so deceiving! I have been so deceived! For years I lied to myself excusing little things that now add up to this BIG mess. I pray God can bring us all out to HIGHER ground, above this mess. Love you all.

Keep praying, this could be a tougher week than (any of) the previous ones.

John

CHAPTER TWENTY-NINE

LEAVING

Thursday, July 10th was set for moving day. I rented a two bedroom apartment in Marion. I did not take much at all except my clothes, personal items and a single mattress, things which fit in my van. My mom helped me set up the apartment and that act of support went a long way to making the first few weeks bearable. By this time, my children were being sent to other homes to spend the night. In the eyes of those in charge, it was too dangerous to allow them to have contact with me. The story continues:

Jul 9, 2008
Mom,
   Martha sent the children away again. I am going to sleep. Get up in AM and write Sarah and Michael a note, tell Martha and pack. This is too much for me.
Love,
John
*****
An email to my brother on July 10th:

   I am moved out. I am sitting at McDonalds drinking a Diet Coke. The song playing was "Betty Lou has a new pair of shoes."

Martha left early, did not wake me. She calls me when she is gone. I told her I would call her back. The children had been farmed out to other houses. I decided to load and then call each person. I loaded, took a shower and walked out to the van. I see Michael watering flowers across the street at a WOFF neighbor!! I was told he was somewhere else. I walk over and tell him I am moving he says "okay" like the sky is blue. NO REACTION. I call Sarah and she is calm almost to the point of simple joy.

I call Martha and she says "It didn't have to be this way."

I say yes, it did not have to be this way. We can talk later. I told each one that they are welcome any time to visit, I have two bedrooms. Well, I was so stupid to expect any other reaction.

Love you—let's talk later about things not associated w/WOFF or my "family."

John

*****

And with that, my life changed forever. The following Monday, Martha put my stuff in the garage in a big pile and told me to come get it. The following email relates that experience.

Jul 14, 2008

Mom,

Well, that was just Weird! Martha was there at the house by herself.

"The children did not want to see you," was the answer to my asking where they are.

We settled a few pending money matters. I told her where I lived, she did admit to wanting to know. I told her to keep in touch, call.

She said, "Why are you doing all this?" Meaning - moving out.

I told her from the question, she was not ready to hear. I did not want any big discussions about who all the parties involved were and what they believed and when I was going to hell or where ever that would have led. So, I gave her a hug. She did at least let me use the restroom while I was there. And she did want to know where I lived, and she does know how to get there.

It has been another emotional day. I may walk twice tomorrow.

More later...

John

*****

In the next email, I add an important point that Martha made during the meeting in the garage.

July 14, 2008

Mom,

The part I forgot to mention was that prior to the, "Why are you doing all this?" Martha again tried to assert that regardless of what I said—I did not love them. Else then the question... Why are you doing all this? So, having in mind her thinking—if you loved us you would be going to church with us—thus my answer from the question, she is not ready to hear the answer.

Hope it makes more sense. I just did not cut her off. She already had the pained look on her face during the "you can't love us" exchange...

*****

The garage meeting struck me hard. In yet another email later that same day, I add to the explanation of how I felt and what I took it all to mean.

Jul 14, 2008

Mom,

As I drove away from Martha and already not seeing the children—not knowing when I would see any of them again. That is a VERY strange feeling. Heavy is not even close to describing it. I am realizing they are headed in their direction, and I am headed in my direction. And at this minute, they are opposites.

Forget for one minute the STRANGE circumstances, I have known her and loved her for 21 years! And now she grimaces when I say "I love you" because we don't attend the same church? Or, in her mind, an even more euphemistic term—you are not "serving God" with us? If it weren't so farfetched and absurd, I would cry more and louder. But, I am still stunned at the thought of us living in 2 different places and she considers me hell bound and going faster every day. I made sure with all I knew to let her know she is welcome at my apartment any time. For God's sake and in His eyes—we are still married. I have nothing to hide. I did not get a 2 bedroom apartment to use the 2nd one for storage. But, I will for now. But, I am trusting God for another bed to use in there. At least set it up for them.

I did get my plants. She had my stuff sitting in the garage when I got there. I can get the sofa, loveseat and chair any time. I told the couple giving them to me, I now have more places to sit than friends to use them.

I need to go…

John

CHAPTER THIRTY

SURVIVING THE SHOCK

The detailed memories of the next few months were tucked away among all the other stored months since my separation from WOFF. I revisited them while researching this book. Again, as a resource, I reviewed the emails sent during that time. The emotions, the restless sleep, working, walking and of course thinking of what had happened over the last few weeks—all of these consumed me.

After suffering intense rejection over the last few weeks, I hesitated to go back for more. My contact efforts with my wife over the next few weeks were sparse. There may have been some text messages. This did not strike me as odd. The message from my family was heart-breaking and clear. We don't want you if you don't want "God." In this case, "God" was the leader and life of WOFF. What other explanation could there be? I had not renounced God; I had renounced faith in and support of WOFF ways and the group leader. My struggle included separating the two in my mind. For years, the dividing line was blurry. As a result, I stayed under the WOFF influence.

I remember the weekdays filled with working at two different Credit Unions and walking for stress relief. In April, the leader had prohibited my exercise walking on church grounds and finding the neighborhood was full of barking dogs, I started walking at the city cemetery in Marion. Yes, it sounds odd, but there were several nice hills. It was quiet. That practice rewarded me with hours to think. I distinctly remember one trip around the cemetery. The question came to me, *Why am I not afraid of the Pope?* The answer was of course, *I am not Catholic. Then why be afraid of the leader of WOFF?, I was no longer a part of WOFF.* This thought went a long way to move me forward in my liberties.

At the end of July, I consulted an attorney. The advice included having my separation agreement in writing. I left that meeting unwilling to believe this situation required legal documents. After all, my wife and I had an understanding. Even though we were not together, we were still together on the matters of the children and the finances, right? My delusion was crushed in the months and years to come. Why did I think I was any different from other spouses who separated from the church? To my discredit, my opinion about my situation was full of fantasy concerning how I would be dealt with by my spouse and the in-house legal counsel of WOFF. My legal education was enhanced by the drama over the next few years.

During those first weeks after the separation, I read a lot. I rediscovered my passion for books and reading until all hours of the night. After reading, *Slave and Citizen – The Life of Frederick Douglass,* by Nathan Irvin Huggins in September, I took notes and planned "editorials" about life inside the group. The passage of the book that struck me included a slave master's comments about the results of teaching a slave to read. I shared this with my mom because of the similarities of the control inside of WOFF.

"Hugh Auld, with course and brutal language told his wife that slaves should never be taught beyond their station. Not only was it illegal to teach a slave to read, but it would "spoil the best n(---)r in the world."... A slave should know nothing but the will of his master. "If you learn him how to read, he'll want to know how to write, and, this accomplished, he'll be running away with himself."[7]

This passage struck a deep chord in me. I knew the group did not keep the members from learning to read or write; however, they did keep regular members from reading and having free unhindered access to information sources which did not repeat the WOFF praises. And try writing something which included doubt about the leader and the methods of the group. You were not even supposed to think those things, much less write them.

Reading this one passage was the catalyst that started me writing my experiences from inside. I purchased the book at a used book store for less than $1.00. It was a providential investment. Over the next few months, I was "running away with myself" telling all I knew about life inside the group. These notes served as the foundation of my first letters to my friends and relatives explaining my circumstances and events of previous years.

Added to my new-found reading sources, the information found on different Internet forums included testimonies of former church members. These were all confirmation to what I had experienced and was still experiencing. Thank you, to any former member who posted on those forums. When finding these sources and others about similar religious cult groups, I shared them with my mom. These times of sharing were the spark for us both to learn more about my experiences and eventually lead her to write *Satan's Best Friend*. Her book is a novel about the making of a cult leader. It is a composite of all the many hours we spent learning and sharing about WOFF, other groups and their leaders. Those times of sharing with her encouraged and supported me in my efforts to break free and live "outside the (WOFF) box."

In September, I reconnected through email with a few dear friends from high school days. This was a vital help for me to rejoin with the lost years which were so demonized by my involvement in WOFF. I later visited my friends. They did not understand all that I had suffered (even I did not at that point), but they were gentle and considerate. We shared laughs remembering school days and youthful events.

During these weeks, my memory and records do not show extensive contact with my wife and children. Why should they? I was under the impression I was not wanted. They shunned me and for that purpose, it worked. I left the home. I did find a reference in September to copying some files off of the laptop and sending them to my wife. She needed them for school work. Other than a few text messages, I don't recall regular communication.

I did not change my cell number or change my mailing address. Even with the confusing circumstances surrounding this break, I loved them and wanted to have contact without the drama.

My ideas were simple to the point of being juvenile during the first few weeks. I bought a medication or cleaning product and thought to myself, before I use all of this, I will be back with my family. Well, I reached the bottom of the container and yet, no reunion with the family I loved. Again, I thought, well, maybe by the time this next jar is empty, there will be a peaceful reunion. After several disappointing views of the bottom of containers, I was forced to give up this fantasy.

During an October trip to visit my high school friends, I was talking with one of them and pointed to my left forearm. There was a growth which had been there for several months, maybe up to a year or more.

"I am going to have that removed soon."

She looked at it. "Good."

Before leaving WOFF, I had covered the growth with a bandage when working out in the sun. Also, I showed it to a nurse in the group who worked for a dermatologist. She gave it a look saying, "It should come off, but it will be okay."

By October, this area grew vertically. All of the drama in the previous months kept me from paying it much attention. But now, it concerned me.

CHAPTER THIRTY-ONE

SEE WHY WE DO THIS
IN A HOSPITAL

The weeks passed, the drama continued.

The Wednesday of the week before Thanksgiving, I visited a surgeon referred by a friend. Once his examination started, he peered and rubbed and looked intently at the spot. I told him just to cut it out. He quickly agreed.

"What are you doing for Thanksgiving?" he asked me.

"I have plans to travel out of town."

"What are you doing the Wednesday after Thanksgiving?"

"Nothing that could not be rearranged."

"The surgery will be that day, in the morning."

I told him I wanted to stay awake for it and he agreed, but said it will be performed in the hospital.

"Why?

"This type of surgery is always better in a hospital."

Well, okay, I was still unaware of the seriousness of the situation.

I told my Mom about the surgery and told my co-workers I may be out for a day. Mom and my stepfather came to be with me during this time. The hospital financial department called a few days before the surgery saying I needed a certain amount of money before they operated. The night before the surgery, I considered not going since I did not have the whole amount and was too prideful to ask for it. But, I went the next morning to the hospital, and we worked out a repayment plan.

I was awake during the surgery, watching the surgeon work with the growth. He extracted it and showed it to me. All of a sudden, I felt light-headed.

The surgeon exclaimed, "Lean him back!"

He sweetly added, "See why we do this in a hospital?"

The next Monday, December 8th, I attended the appointment to review the pathology results. The nurse led me back to the surgeon's office. He motioned for me to sit and closed the door.

He explained, "There are three types of skin cancer. Basil, squamous and melanoma, unfortunately you have malignant melanoma."

He chuckled. I was not sure why he chuckled except to ease the confused look on my face.

"We will need to go back in and take out more tissue from your forearm. We may need to take out lymph nodes. The surgery will be next Wednesday morning. The nurse will give you an appointment time for pre-op and your instructions. After the surgery, we will know the need for treatment options. Do you have any questions?"

Questions? Of course, I had no questions. I did not know enough to have questions.

He was now serious, no chuckles. I felt overwhelmed by the unknown. After getting my information packet, I walked to my van, stunned. I called Mom and told her the report.

She said, "I will be there for you."

"Is this serious? I have not researched anything."

"Don't look this up on the Internet!" she said. "You don't need to know right now."

"Okay. I won't."

The next few days flew by as I prepared for the unknown. Three days later, I broke my promise and researched melanoma. The information was sobering. This diagnosis was even more serious than the heart attack.

Among other things, I hoped to avoid my wife for a few weeks. I knew she would see this as evidence of God's judgment for my leaving WOFF. As crazy as that sounded, I struggled with it myself for a little while until I remembered the cancer appeared while I lived inside. The drama of the last few months had diverted my attention from the seriousness of the growth and delayed my trip to the surgeon.

Mom and others came to support me before and after the surgery. The operation took longer than originally anticipated. A dear friend from work came to support my mom. Finally, the surgeon emerged into the waiting area to give the report.

"I had to remove six lymph nodes, the process was difficult. I believe I got it all."

Somewhere during the recovery time, the doctor came to me and explained his findings. I remember his face and some of his words but was glad my mom heard the full report. After more lab results, we planned to discuss treatment options.

During the days and weeks following the surgery, my emotions were intense. On the one hand, I did not want to tell my wife, on the other hand, I desperately needed the support and love I thought she could and would provide. Ultimately, this turmoil led me to go to her house and knock on the front door. In the letter she sent after my visit, she recounts the confusing messages from me. One day, I told her I was glad we were talking, on another day; I said I was seeking legal counsel. I remember standing on her doorstep that day in December, as she wearily walked to the door explaining she had been in sick and in bed.

She opened the door and I blurted out, "Are you through with me?"

She replied, "What are you talking about?"

She may have said other things, I don't recall. The confusion and fear over my illness added to the ongoing implosion of a twenty-year marriage caused me to withdraw from the encounter without asking for the very thing I needed most -- love and support. Deep down, I feared another round of rejection overlaid with spiritual sounding catch phrases, which to me were a barrier too high jump over. During those days, I experienced confusion and fear of the unknown. My arm and leg were healing, but my heart was continually torn apart. The family I loved rejected me over the very religion I had previously defended.

CHAPTER THIRTY-TWO

TRIP TO GEORGIA

A few days later, with my arm and leg in bandages, I rented a car and took off to Georgia to visit relatives for Christmas, my first Christmas season outside of the group. The warm reception by all was comforting. Everyone overlooked my awkwardness as we went through the normal Christmas family traditions. Yes, I remembered the traditions, though I had not practiced them in years. I had lived "locked-in" to the non-traditions of WOFF and now was learning to live "unlocked." Learning to live away from the group takes time.

I appreciated all of the people around me who gave me time and space during those first few months to learn who I was and what I believed. It has been and continues to be a process.

As 2008 closed, there was no lack of drama for me. Yet, there were many people and things to be grateful for. I reunited with my parents and siblings as well as extended family and friends. My medical condition was diagnosed and treatment was starting in a few weeks. This was a blessing which I did not fully comprehend.

As I faced 2009, who could predict the new things I would learn? I was on a course to learn about melanoma treatments and family law. All of these experiences, and the new friends I met along the way, helped me live *free* from the controls inside WOFF.

EPLILOGUE

There was no way to tell when I moved my wife and daughter from Summerville, SC to Greenville, SC in March of 1992 that eventually our family would separate over the teachings and practices of WOFF. Who knew in 2002, Jane Whaley would "hear from God" that the Greenville church was to move to Spindale, NC? After we moved in 2002, our lives were on a fast track to become part of the statistics of broken families as a result of WOFF.

By writing this account, I do not pretend to have all the answers. My healing journey continues and the learning has not stopped. During my time inside, questions were not encouraged, specifically questions about Jane, her authority and her decisions. The writing of this book has been a way to bring out the many stifled questions which were buried through the years. During this writing process, I examined certain decisions and choices. This has been good for me. I hope sharing my doubts and weaknesses increases the understanding of the emotional toll of life inside WOFF.

It took several years to get past the initial exit and personal trauma of leaving so I could face what happened. The writing of this book does not mean the WOFF saga is finished. In fact, this book only indicates a pause in the road, a time of reflection. There seems to be enough time away from that group for me to accurately look back and tell what I saw, what I heard and what I experienced. This book was not written to garner pity but to explain my struggles and my victories.

I found no written manual on how to exit a high-demand faith group or religious cult. It took several months to even admit that I had been under mind control and needed some help to readjust to life outside WOFF. In January of 2010, with the help of my brother, I started a blog. That step made a big difference in my recovery. On the blog, I shared my experiences inside and what I learned about those experiences. By writing the posts, I pieced together how I entered into this group. Many resource books for my blog posts served as learning guides. I started the process of sorting out the experiences and understanding the methods of influence used on me. After I crossed the hurdle of admitting how traumatic the WOFF experience was, then the idea of telling my story made sense.

Thank you, for taking the time to purchase and read my story. You can access more about my journey and send questions or comments through my blog, www.religiouscultsinfo.com, or my website, www.johnhuddle.net. Look for the sequel online at major book sellers or through my website.

Footnotes:

[1] Modisett, Bill. "Shelter from the Storm." OA Online. Odessa American, 14 June 2008. Web. 2 May 2015. <http://www.oaoa.com>.

[2] Cuneo, Michael W. American Exorcism: Expelling Demons in the Land of Plenty. New York: Doubleday, 2001. Print.

[3] Trinity Foundation – Word of Faith Fellowship/Inside Edition – link: https://www.youtube.com/watch?v=YwE5fBT9RYE- viewed May 2, 2015

[4] Word of Faith Fellowship Vs. Rutherford County Dept of Social Services. Western District of North Carolina Asheville Division. 10 June 2004. Web. 2 May 2015. http://law.justia.com/cases/federal/district-courts/FSupp2/329/675/2410161/ Civil Action 1:03CV298.

[5] Hassan, Steven. "Chapter 4." Combatting Cult Mind Control. Rochester, VT: Park Street, 1988. 53. Print.www.freedomofmind.com

[6] Johnson, David, and Jeffrey VanVonderen. "Identifying the Abusive System - Unspoken Rules." The Subtle Power of Spiritual Abuse. Minneapolis, MN: Bethany House, 1991. 67. Print.

[7] Huggins, Nathan Irvin, and Oscar Handlin. "In Every Man the Spark." Slave and Citizen: The Life of Frederick Douglass. Boston: Little, Brown, 1980. 5. Print.

Glossary:

1. **Take hold** – This phrase could mean- shape up. Get with the program! Put a lid on it. Just obey what you have been told. The phrase meant different things according to the context. "Take hold of that person" meant help them "get their heart right" and submitting to whatever Jane said or some new rule.

2. **Open your Heart**, - Share your heart, and share those very personal thoughts and desires. Tell ALL your sin to someone who is "taking hold of your life". This practice eventually led to someone in leadership having the scoop on you and reminding you of this at some point in the future. Of course, used in a spiritual way to mold your behavior to meet the WOFF standards.

3. **Locked in**- Are you locked in? Stay locked in. Be sure to lock in before you do whatever it is you want to do. This phrase meant different things at different times. There were different applications of the root meaning. At the foundation was submitting to Jane or someone in leadership your ideas about a decision or question before you made the final decision. Locking in also meant letting others know where you were at all times. Living locked in was evident because you obeyed all the rules and never were "out from under authority" or on your own –doing your own thing. (free) It was a compliment to be told you were locked in about a situation. Staying locked in included physically calling someone at certain intervals while you were on a trip or out of physical contact with another WOFF member. Families on trips to see relatives were expected to "lock in" on the phone about the contact with relatives or other exposures to worldly things. Faithful

members showed their loyalty by "locking in" over the smallest details or their inner thoughts which might pull them away from God. Thoughts which cause them to think negatively about WOFF or Jane. If you did not lock in, you were in rebellion and hiding sin and could be on your way to hell.

4. **"Fulfill your call"**- This one phrase was sung in songs and used to exhort members to aspire to the ever moving standard of submission to each new rule or edict. In some cases, this meant becoming more obedient or "fulfilling your call", you would move up the ranks, passing the control on to others of lesser rank in the WOFF social pyramid. You were to repeat the daily message or theme until others got it through you. It was said many times; "You will never full your call until you help someone else fulfill their call." The way this transpired was you finding someone else to "help open their heart" and "take hold of them". Help them "find their place of submission in Jesus", or in the group- which ever was more obvious.

5. **"Stay submitted"**- This phrase was a warning, meaning don't get mad about something that you don't understand, even if the matter was obviously going contrary to common sense. Also, don't ask any more questions about it. Staying submitted included being reminded to "be sweet". One leader spent several sermons talking about how he was learning to **"be sweet"** and how that helped him. In effect, he caught fewer fits of wrath by being sweet and agreeing to everything he was told to do.

6. **"Fine tuning"** - Did you get fine tuning on that? This question meant getting further instruction or interpretation on

a situation from Jane. You were not able to decide on your own about your life, you could not "hear clearly because of the sin in your life…" It was a spiritual way to call someone "less spiritual" or lower on the pyramid.

7. **"Work Projects"**- Participating in these meant taking time after normal work hours and on Saturdays to work at someone else's house helping them. It could also be at the church or on a church owned property. There was a list that Jane and one of her close helpers kept of houses needing paint, carpet, or other changes. Early on, many men were told they needed to get involved in these work projects ESPECIALLY if they had handyman skills. I painted for a while until it was obvious that doing this left little to no time for family activities. (In some cases- men were told they "gave to perversion" with their family so, why would you need to spend much time with them?") Getting involved in helping others would "help you come into your place in the ministry." It made you so tired, you could not think logically.

8. **"Receiving a Blessing"**- Your "blessing" could have a big mortgage payment or even a large car payment attached to it. Sounded to me like a strange blessing. Anything which may be evidence of a prosperous lifestyle had to be a blessing in the WOFF kind of way. This was all part of the culture.

9. **"Go get checked out"** - Members were encouraged to "go get checked out" to see if they were hearing right. This meant meeting with Jane Whaley to find out if she agrees with whatever choice or decision you were making. Jane claimed to pray about and listen to God for direction for your life. If she was not "hearing what you were hearing," then you were automatically wrong.

10. **"That did not feel right"**. The phrase means different things at different times. Most of the time, someone used this phrase to arrest the attention of others concerning something they did or said. This might involve an individual or a group of folks and by using the phrase; you were putting them on notice that the whole situation was now going to be reviewed by someone in leadership, most likely, Jane. Then it could be checked out to see if everyone involved was "giving to Jesus" and "had a hold of Jesus" and other such spiritual sounding phrases. Many times it was a whole big deal and new doctrines, rules and edicts came from using this one phrase. These sessions became an exhibition of Jane's power to determine what was sin; who was in sin; who was right and who was "giving to devils" and further clarification of who was in charge.

These terms and others permeated the communication inside WOFF. Listing the unique phrases used in WOFF-speak proves difficult because there were so many. Over the years, some fell out of use and new ones were spawned. Naturally, since my departure, new phrases have been created and others are not used as much. The unique language of this group spawned a sense of pride and camaraderie one would expect to be needed in order to withstand the internal demands of membership. This special language became so engrained in members that upon their exit, there is a purposeful searching to learn phrases used by non-members. Former members often find a sense of comfort when speaking to other former members, because they are more easily understood.

Resources:

Books:

Hassan, Steven. *Freedom of Mind: Helping Loved Ones Leave Controlling People, Cults and Beliefs*. Newton, MA: Freedom of Mind, 2012. Print.

Hill, Jenna Miscavige, and Lisa Pulitzer. *Beyond Belief: My Secret Life inside Scientology and My Harrowing Escape*. New York: Harper Collins, 2013. Print.

Jeffs, Brent W., and Maia Szalavitz. *Lost Boy- This Is My Story*. New York: Broadway, 2009. Print.

Jessop, Flora, and Paul T. Brown. *Church of Lies*. San Francisco: Jossey-Bass, 2009. Print. This book inspired me in January 2010.

Jessop, Carolyn, and Laura Palmer. *Escape*. New York: Broadway, 2007. Print.

Langone, Michael D., ed. *Recovery from Cults: Help for Victims of Psychological and Spiritual Abuse*. New York: W.W. Norton, 1993. Print. Great Resource!

Lifton, Robert Jay. *Thought Reform and the Psychology of Totalism: A Study of "brainwashing" in China*. Chapel Hill: U of North Carolina, 1989. Print. Chapter 22 of this book is very helpful in understanding mind control in dangerous groups.

Wall, Elissa, and Lisa Pulitzer. *Stolen Innocence*. New York: Harper Collins, 2008. Print. Inspiring.

Websites:

http://culteducation.com/group/1232-word-of-faith-fellowship.html - resource of newspaper articles concerning Word of Faith Fellowship, very valuable.

http://freedomofmind.com- Steven Hassan website is an extensive resource.

http://www.icsahome.com/ - International Cultic Studies Association- online resources, conferences, sessions, educational materials and connections for those seeking help after time in a dangerous group or relationship.

STATE OF NORTH CAROLINA

COUNTY OF RUTHERFORD

WAIVER & RELEASE

Waiver & Release agreement executed by _____, of
_____, City of _____
County of _____, State of _____, as releasor, to The
Word of Faith Fellowship, Inc., a non-profit religious organization, existing under the laws of the State of
North Carolina, with its principal office on Old Flynn Road. in Spindale, North Carolina 28160,
previously located on U.S. Highway 221, Rutherfordton, North Carolina, its directors, officers, agents,
employees, and any other person connected therewith, particularly the pastor or pastors of The Word of
Faith Fellowship, Inc.

Now, therefore, for and in consideration of the sum of One and No/100 Dollar ($1.00), paid by the party of
the first part to the party of the second part and by the party of the second part to the party of the first part,
the receipt of which is hereby acknowledged, said parties agree as follows:

1. The Word of Faith Fellowship, Inc. is a legally existing organized church and is recognized as such by
the State of North Carolina and the United States Government;

2. That The Word of Faith. Fellowship, Inc. is a charismatic Evangelical church which believes in the
Holy Bible as the true and living Word of God; that it believes in speaking in tongues, casting out devils
and divine healing, as taught by the Word of God and as part of its worship services. The Word of Faith
Fellowship, Inc., its agents, employees, members and other participants taking part in the worship services
at said church, do speak in tongues, do have deliverance, do have healing services, do have casting out
devils services and in most of the usual and normal services as are carried on in charismatic evangelical
churches;

3 That no guarantee or warranty of any kind is made to releasor or to any other party that demons or devils
will be cast out; that their bodies will be healed; that their' souls will be saved or that their mental and/or
emotional condition will be cured; that the parties of the second part do not hold out that they have any
education nor practice whatsoever in psychiatry, psychology, mental counseling, marital counseling, nor
are they experts in any field whatsoever that might have to do with the spirit or the physical thing of a
person, except that which is taught in the Word of God; they make claim whatsoever, should a person
receive healing, deliverance, spirit filling or any other condition that they will not digress from this
condition and return to their old condition;

That all the healings, casting out of demons and deliverance are done through prayer and ministry of the
Word of God.

I, _____ - , have requested that the parties of the second part, their directors, officers, agents, employees
or any other person connected therewith work with me to the end that I may receive the blessing which
God may have for me through prayer and ministry of the Word of God, be it through deliverance, healing,
casting out demons or anything else which might happen to me during ministry at The Word of. Faith
Fellowship, Inc. recently located at 511 Old Flynn Road, Spindale, North Carolina 28160.

I have been informed of all the above statements and have read them and understand each and every one of
them. I hereby release the pastors and the persons connected with The Word of Faith Fellowship, Inc,

severally and individually, from any and all liability of any nature or kind, for whatever injury or harm or complication of any kind that may result whether directly or indirectly by reason of my subjecting myself to prayers and ministry during any services of the parties, of the second part.

I hereby waive any and all rights of action I may have or later acquire as a result of the condition as it exists at the date of this signing and may re occur hereafter

I also waive my right of any action for money damages resulting from so called spiritual, mental, financial, emotional, physical, social, or loss, suffered as a result of any ministry given me by any person associated directly or indirectly with The Word of Faith Fellowship, Inc., including ministry received by me from visitors.

I understand that in some spiritual atmospheres there may be some mind control involved,. however, after witnessing the ministry and atmosphere of The Word of Faith Fellowship, Inc., I believe that the pastors and other persons connected with The Word of Faith Fellowship, Inc. do not operate in mind control; they operate in the power and anointing of God.

I have discussed this document with the Reverend Sam G. Whaley, Jr. and/or Reverend Jane B. Whaley or an employee of The Word of Faith Fellowship, Inc., and they have explained to me, in detail, what is going to take place. I have been advised by the Reverends Whaley and/or other agents of The Word of Faith Fellowship, Inc. that it is my duty, if I do not understand this document, to take it to a lawyer of my choice, before executing this Agreement.

I fully understand this Agreement and what it means. This Agreement is made with. my full knowledge of its content and am fully aware of the danger that arises out of any mental or spiritual exorcism.

I, also, as legal guardian of the minor children listed below do waive any right or claim or lawsuit based on any principle of law pertaining to any ministry given to my children by the pastors or any other person connected with The Word of Faith Fellowship, Inc.

Name of Minor Child Birth date Name of Minor Child Birth date

The staff of The Word of Faith Fellowship, Inc. hereby agree to give their best effort to minister to
_____ as consideration for this Agreement.

IN WITNESS WHEREOF, releasor executes this Agreement at Spindale, North Carolina on the
_____ day of _____, 19

Sam G. Whaley, Pastor and President of the Board

Jane B. Whaley, Pastor

Signature

Name (Please Print)

* *

STATE OF NORTH CAROLINA

COUNTY OF RUTHERFORD

(SEAL)

I,_____ A Notary Public of said County and State, do hereby certify that personally appeared before me this day and acknowledged the execution of the foregoing agreement.

Witness my hand and notarial seal this day of_____ 19

(SEAL)

My commission expires

Notary Public

Page 2

ABOUT THE AUTHOR

John Huddle continues to live in Western North Carolina. He works providing services to Credit Unions. In addition to writing his blog, www.religiouscultsinfo.com, John serves as a member of the Faith Freedom Fund helping survivors from high demand religious groups. He is also a member of the International Cultic Studies Associations (ICSA). John attended their annual conference in July 2014 held in Washington, D.C. There he read the Prologue to this book and it was well received, garnering mention in their first magazine published in 2015. Membership in this Association allows John to meet and connect with survivors from many different types of high-demand groups, gaining from their experiences and friendship. Look for John's next book revealing the struggles and victories after leaving WOFF, expected to be published in 2016.

Made in the USA
Lexington, KY
30 September 2015